TEXAS RHYTHM

TEXAS RHYME

A PICTORIAL HISTORY OF TEXAS MUSIC

BY LARRY WILLOUGHBY

Tonkawa Free Press

Published in 1984 by Texas Monthly Press

Tonkawa Free Press
P.O. Box 12543
Austin, Texas 78711

A   B   C   D   E   F   G   H

Library of Congress Cataloging in Publication Data

Willoughby, Larry,
    Texas rhythm, Texas rhyme.

    Includes index.
    1. Music, Popular (Songs, etc.)—Texas—History and criticism—Pictorial works. I. Title.
ML3477.W6   1984   789'.42'09764   83-24234
ISBN   0-89015-802-9

A Juneteenth musical celebration, circa 1900. *(Austin History Center)*

The gravesite of Texas' foremost musical legend—located at an eastside Lubbock cemetery. *(Courtesy of Bill Griggs, Buddy Holly Memorial Society)*

Willie Nelson's Fourth of July Picnic, 1979. *(Scott Newton)*

A psychedelic lightshow at the Vulcan Gas Company in Austin, 1970—Shiva's Headband in performance. *(Burton Wilson)*

Table of Contents

Poster advertising the Texas International Pop Festival near Lewisville, 1969. *(Texas Music Collection)*

The last Soap Creek Saloon calendar from June, 1981—artist Kerry Awn. *(Texas Music Collection)*

A Rolling Stones dance was held every Wednesday in Hondo during the early 1950s. *(Courtesy of Leon Carter)*

Artist Jim Franklin's painting of Freddie King at the Armadillo World Headquarters. *(Texas Music Collection)*

Pickin' the country blues—Mance Lipscomb, Bill Neely, and Taj Mahal. *(Burton Wilson)*

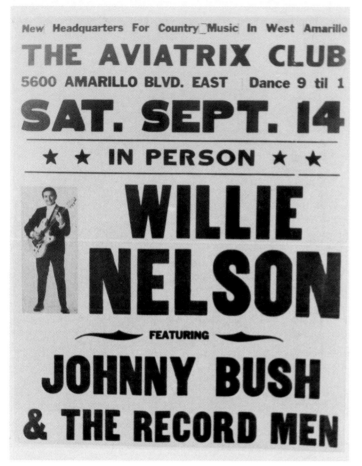

Promotion for a Willie Nelson concert in the 1960s at the Aviatrix Club, Amarillo. *(Texas Music Collection)*

Antone's—Home of the Blues. Austin. *(Susan Antone)*

Backstage at the filming of the documentary film on conjunto music, *Chulas Fronteras*, featuring Narciso Martinez with his accordion. *(Chris Strachwitz)*

Acknowledgments

The photographs that compose this pictorial history came from a wide variety of souces — institutions, collectors, record companies, professional photographers, and a great number of individuals. I am indebted to all of you who contributed pictures, information, or inspiration to this effort.

For their cooperation and expert assistance, I would like to extend my gratitude to the staffs of the following musical or historical archives: the John Edwards Memorial Foundation at UCLA, the University of Texas Institute of Texan Cultures at San Antonio, the Country Music Foundation in Nashville, and the Barker Texas History Center at the University of Texas. I also received invaluable support from Arhoolie Records, Warner Brothers Records, MCA Records, CBS Records, and *Living Blues* magazine.

My greatest debt in assembling this book is to all the individual photographers and collectors who provided photographs — a special thanks to Burton Wilson, Rick Henson, Scott Newton, Brian Kanof, Leon and Chic Carter, Huey Meaux, Doug Hanners, Charles Townsend, Chuck Gist, George and Carlyne Majewski, David Fox, Dennie Tarner, Chris Strachwitz, Duncan Schiedt, Diana and Paul Ray, Bill Griggs, Clay Shorkey, Jim Willis, Scott VanOsdol, Jane Stader, Al Dressen, Susan Antone, John Carrico, and Jeff Rowe. Others who provided insight and assistance include Bobby and Ray Schultz, Jane and Brad Dobervich, Tim and Linda Smythe, Butch McCrary, Claude Matthews, Robyn Turner, Ellen Simmons, Ed Eakin, Earl and Janie Fields, and Suzanne Wright. My appreciation is also extended to Rod Kennedy and all the artists, staff, and fans at the Kerrville Folk Festival.

The inspiration for this project came, of course, from the performers who make the music. A great many people shared that music and gave it meaning, so a final acknowledgment to my friends who advised, supported, and helped me stay off Maggie's Farm.

A jazz dance band, circa 1920s. *(Austin History Center)*

Advertisement for one of Blind Lemon Jefferson's Paramount recordings in the 1920s—"Lectric Chair Blues." *(Texas Music Collection)*

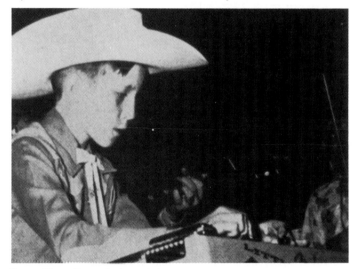

Future Texas Tornado Doug Sahm at age eleven. *(Texas Music Collection)*

A Sunday morning service at Chapel Hill, Kerrville Folk Festival. The Kerrville Festival celebrates its twentieth anniversary in 1991. *(Jim Willis)*

Preface

While promoting the first edition of this book, I was repeatedly asked by interviewers, reviewers, and readers to "tell us about your book on country music." I politely replied with a frustrated response: *"Texas Rhythm, Texas Rhyme* covers country music, of course, but it also includes all the musical styles that have developed throughout the last century—folk, blues, jazz, swing, and rock. My book is about much more than country music; it's about Texas music."

Following my spiel on the diversity and breadth of the Texas musical experience, the interested critic ended the interview with an obligatory, "Thank you for sharing your observations on your country music book." Obviously, many Texans still cling to the time-worn images and culturally nourished stereotypes that limit the vision of who and what constitutes "Texan."

To counter that narrow view of "Texas music," this second edition of *Texas Rhythm, Texas Rhyme* has an updated Epilogue that includes a vast variety of artists. Rock stars, country performers, and blues artists—all are portrayed in the same pictorial presentation. To reiterate the philosophical theme of the book, I include the original preface as follows . . .

An Austin April often brings more than bluebonnets and hill country rain. During the early 1970s the first signs of Texas summer brought outdoor music festivals to the lakeside pastures and the oak-covered fields surrounding Austin. For thousands of Texans those concerts were the staple of their social diet—a ritual steeped in the tradition of Texas chauvinism and youthful rebellion. An incident at one such outing near Bull Creek Party Barn, a few miles northwest of Austin, gave rise to an ironic fascination that proved to be the genesis of this book.

As Jerry Jeff Walker and the Lost Gonzo Band smoothly moved from country melody to a two-minute rock riff, a sun-baked observer with twelve empty Lone Stars in his cooler irreverently growled, "What are you playing, Walker, country or rock?" I was uncertain whether Jerry Jeff's critic wanted more fiddle or more hard metal, but I was certain that the question was a valid one. For I had grown up on rock 'n' roll, and the line between rock and country was a very distinct one for a Texas Panhandle refugee of the 1960s. It was a line that separated the sophisticated from the provincial, the enlightened from the redneck, the future from the past. But after my baptism in the hybrid Austin sound of that period, it became apparent that I was naive about Texas music, and in fact, naive about the land and people that gave it birth. This book is the culmination of a ten-year attempt to re-educate myself, to explore the rich and exciting social and cultural heritage of a Texas that I had not known and had not understood.

While discovering my version of that ambiguous concept, "Texas music," I repeatedly faced the dilemma posed by the Texas legend, or more accurately, the Texas myth. The stereotypes and the clichés abound—the big, brash, boastful Texan, decked out in alligator skin boots with hundred-dollar bills gushing from his pockets as fast as oil from his private well. He is a wheeler-dealer from North Dallas, lives in a man's world full of obedient, perfumed women, and has a code of ethics defined by profit-and-loss statements. He has his rural counterpart—the good ol' boy from West Texas who equates rock with revolution and pickups with patriotism.

Unfortunately, the American public's image of Texas music, and even the perception of most Texans, follows a similar scenario. The generalizations usually begin with terms like *redneck, kicker, honky-tonk,* and they always seem to end with the musical macho of the urban cowboy. But Texas music defies the simplistic stereotypes that have plagued it since commercial popular music began in the 1920s. It is a diverse and complex art form that sprang from a diverse and complex people. Those who limit its scope with racist labels or pseudo-sophisticated phrases have made the music victim of society's most vicious social disease, intolerance. The Texas musicians who fill the pages of this book rejected intolerance in their search to entertain and to create, and in doing so, they provided American culture a unique and truly democratic institution. It is on this premise that this survey of Texas music is based. The purpose of this pictorial history is threefold: to chronicle the tremendous number of Texas musicians, to acknowledge the contributions of the Texas musicians to the various styles of American popular music, and to portray in one volume all the diverse elements that comprise Texas music: folk, ragtime, country, blues, jazz, swing, and rock.

Despite the misconceptions and the exaggerations surrounding Texas and its people, it obviously has a noble and intriguing historical tradition. And Texas music is no exception to that reality. The music has paralleled the social, cultural, and even economic development of the state. It has symbolized those qualities that are heir to a legitimate Texas heritage—the triumphs and failures of all the Texas people. But putting analytical and critical perspectives aside, the music of Texas has served a higher purpose; it has provided pleasure. And in doing so, it has served well the message inscribed on the banjo of a Texas minstrel who wandered across the Panhandle fifty years ago: "This machine surrounds hate and destroys it."

Scott Joplin—the "Father of Ragtime." This 1912 photo was the last one taken of Joplin, America's greatest composer of the ragtime era. *(Texas Music Collection.)*

1

The Nineteenth-Century Tradition

There's a yellow rose in Texas

There's a yellow rose in Texas
That I am going to see.
Nobody else could miss her
Not half as much as me.
Her eyes are bright as diamonds
They sparkle like the dew.
She's the sweetest little rosebud
That Texas ever knew.

The Yellow Rose of Texas
Nineteenth-century folk song

The music of Texas emanated from America's most diverse ethnic environment and evolved within America's most diverse geographical region. For a century and a half it has served as entertainment, art, and social expression for six generations of Texans. The cultural development of those Texans occured in a geographic maze — a point on the American frontier where there was a convergence of the cotton fields and pine forests of the South, the mountains and deserts of the West, and the high plains and rolling prairies of the Midwest. Within that unique physical setting the acculturation of a variety of ethnic strains took place during the nineteenth century. Texas music emerged from that musical melting pot and became one of the most dynamic and creative forces in American social history. Its sound serves as an anthem to the Texas spirit; its lyrics read like a novel of the American experience.

The music of the early Texans was synonymous with celebration — of faith, country, culture, and the individual. From the battle cadences of the Texas Revolution to the revival hymns on the banks of the Brazos, music was a pervasive presence in the lives of the men and women on the Texas frontier. There was violent confrontation on that frontier among the Indians, Anglos, Mexicans, Germans, Swedes, Cajun French, and Afro-Americans, but there was

also an interaction between them, a borrowing of culture and a sharing of custom. Music was the catalyst for that interaction and the resulting cultural assimilation. Music was the one social institution that reinforced the humanity of all Texans.

After Texas achieved its sovereignty from Mexico in 1836, four identifiable musical traditions were present in Texas society: the folk and religious music of the Texas Indian tribes; a large body of religious hymns and spirituals brought by Texans of the Catholic and Protestant faiths; a European classical heritage that had been imported to Texas from the urban centers of the United States; and folk music rooted in the various rural sounds of the American South. The synthesis of these four musical elements sowed the seeds in Texas for the birth of commercial popular music in the twentieth century.

Even though the contributions of the American Indian to our modern institutions are often ignored, the fact remains that the music of the Indian was the first music in Texas. Each of the different Texas Indian tribes (there were at least twenty distinct Indian nations within Texas' borders) incorporated music into their social and religious lives to a greater degree than the Europeans and the Americans who invaded their homeland. The Texas Indians sang songs of harvest,

1

battle, birth, and death. Their music accentuated the challenges of attaining adulthood and the pride of reaching old age. Music was also the basic foundation for Indian religious ceremonies, usually taking the form of mystical worship ballads and ceremonial dance songs. But the most consistent theme of the Indian music was the land and the water — a message from each generation to the next emphasizing their responsibility to revere and preserve the natural bounty that sustains life.

The first musical collaboration between the Spanish and the Texas Indians took place in the Catholic missions. Prayers were often taught to the Indians and Spanish soldiers to the tunes of native chants and to the accompaniment of guitars, flutes, and drums. *(Drawing by José Cisneros, courtesy Mrs. Cleofas Calleros. University of Texas Institute of Texan Cultures at San Antonio.)*

T he music of the Texas Indians was characterized by its rhythmic beat and its limited instrumentation. Most of the instruments were percussion: drums, rattles, notched sticks. In addition, some tribes had flutelike instruments resembling recorders or whistles. The songs of the nomadic tribes (the Comanches, Kiowa, and Pawnee of the Panhandle and plains region) sounded harsh, with high-pitched and strongly accented tones. In contrast, the Caddoes of East Texas and the Tonkawas of Central Texas had a more soothing, more melodic sound with a narrower range of pitch and a greater emphasis on lyrics. A great deal of Indian religious and folk music survived the nineteenth century in its original form. However, two centuries of close contact between Indians and the Spanish, and the subsequent modifications of both cultures, played a significant role in the development of southwestern folk music, most

notably in the music of the Tejanos (Texans of Mexican origin).

The second category of musical expression in nineteenth-century Texas grew from the religious institutions that were such an integral part of society. The first church music in Texas was heard in the Spanish missions when Catholic priests moved across the Rio Grande in the late 1600s. In addition to prayer books, the priests brought organs and hymnals to aid them in spreading the word to both the Indians of the region and the Spanish soldiers stationed there. The conquistadors had subjugated and enslaved the Texas Indian tribes, and the priests then taught them to sing the songs of their new savior. Often the mission music was a strange combination of Catholic hymns and Tonkawa, or Caddo, or Apache spiritual chants. The relationship between Spanish and Indian musical styles and preferences became an extremely close one, as evidenced by this 1767 observation of a Spanish priest quoted in Lota Spell's *Music in Texas:*

> Most of these Indians play some musical
> instrument, the guitar, the violin or harp.
> All have good voices, and on the days of
> our Lord they take out their rosaries,
> while a choir of four voices, soprano,
> alto, tenor, and bass, with musical accom-
> paniment, sings so beautifully it is a
> delight. Both men and women can sing
> and dance just as the Spaniards, and they
> do so, perhaps, even more beautifully and
> gracefully.

The Protestants began arriving in Texas in the 1820s, and just as their political institutions soon took control, their religious music quickly dominated the social life of Texas. The pride of every congregation was its choir, and competition among the various denominations was documented as early as 1831. There were sacred music societies formed in Austin and Houston in the 1840s, and many of these "professional choirs" continued to flourish in other Texas cities throughout the remainder of the century. One such nondenominational organization, the Sacred Harp Singing Society, is still in existence and still produces unique and eloquent religious folk sounds. The Protestants also created singing schools to promote musical skills among the Texas youth, with many of the graduates later turning to more secular musical tastes. Camp meetings, religious conventions with music as the focal point of the worship service, were the predecessors of the twentieth-century tent revivals where music is used to work believers into a religious frenzy. Religious chauvinism was also a part of the early musical experience in Texas. The lyrics to this Methodist hymn serve as a tongue-in-cheek example:

> ***The devil hates the Methodists***
> ***Because they sing and shout the best,***
> ***And when I die I'll go to rest,***
> ***And live among the Methodists.***

One of the greatest contributors to American folk and popular music has been the black spiritual and gospel song. Although black and white Protestants borrowed heavily from each other, there were distinct differences in the lyrical content of their hymns as well as in the usage of song as part of the worship service. The black churches infused a great deal of African tradition into their music, and of course, the slave legacy was omnipresent in shaping the philosophy and mood of the sermon and the supporting songs. Whereas white Protestants sang to the glories of God and the blessings of life on earth, the black Protestants asked the Lord for help to make it to the next world. Sacrifice, patience, and hope for a better day dominated the lyrics of the black religious community. That hope gave rise to the energy, emotion, and excitement that years later formed the basis of ragtime, jazz, rhythm and blues, and rock 'n' roll.

Religion exposed more Texans to musical training and inspiration than any other nineteenth-century institution. Similarly, the third broad musical category of that era, classical music, played an important role in the training of young Texas musicians. Even though professional symphony orchestras did not appear in Texas until after the Civil War, classical schools and teachers could be found in every Texas city. Classical concerts were held in Texas as early as 1837, the first having been held in Houston at the capitol of the Republic of Texas. There were several Texans who gained national reputations in the classical field: director and composer Franz van der Stucken, composer and performer Harold Morris, turn-of-the-century composers John Steinfeldt and Carl Venth, and classical religious composer William Marsh, best known for writing the state song, *Texas, Our Texas.* Most classical devotees were found in the urban areas, but unlike the experience in other sections of the country, classical training and interest were not limited to just the upper class. Opera companies also found a receptive audience in the larger Texas communities. Dallas, Austin, and San Antonio had regular opera performances as early as 1850. The opera was Texas society's main tie to drama and classical music. The proliferation of classical exposure ended during the early 1900s when many of today's symphony orchestras were formed. The classical tradition in Texas has never rivaled the success achieved in other American locales, but it continues to provide training and

discipline for future Texas musicians.

The last and largest category of nineteenth-century Texas music is the folk song. Folk music is usually defined as music of the common people or songs for the working class. Such songs are passed from one generation to another and are usually of anonymous origin. Woody Guthrie, America's foremost folk singer who spent the 1930s perfecting his craft in the dust-scarred Texas Panhandle, described folk music more succinctly as "music sung by folks, for folks, about folks." It was folk music that most accurately revealed the people and their day-to-day experiences, and it was the music that would most closely resemble the Texas sound of the next century.

Texas folk music, and in fact the folk music of the South, represented a rejection of the European heritage of aristocratic domination of the arts. It was a democratic music that evolved on a frontier seething with opportunity, as well as oppression—a frontier that rewarded individualism, as well as conformity. There were racism, sexism, and bigotry on the democratic frontier where the American South and West collided, but music transcended ethnic, religious, and class differences. Three streams of immigrants provided the cultural mix that produced this Texas folk-song tradition. There were the Tejanos from Mexico, the Americans of European ancestry, and the Americans of African descent.

The lyrics and instrumentation of Texas folk music were as varied as the people who created and enjoyed it. The Mexican population of the southern and western parts of the state borrowed heavily from both the Spanish and the Indians. The Spanish guitar was their instrument of choice, and many of their folk ballads were based on Indian values and beliefs. Mexican folk songs were usually labeled "romantic," in that they often dealt with emotion, religion, or family. But there were also a great many Mexican folk songs that incorporated dancing, holiday celebrations, and children's games. The most enduring Mexican folk songs are the *corridos* (old bal-

The American settlers who began the migration into Texas during the 1820s brought with them a wide array of folk traditions and customs, such as this "flatboat fiddler." (*Drawing from* Frank Leslies' Illustrated Newspaper, *v. 50, 3 April 1880, p. 82. University of Texas Institute of Texan Cultures at San Antonio.*)

Music has traditionally been a barometer of class distinction and social status. Since most Texans of the nineteenth century were frontier farmers, their folk music was considered crude and unrefined by the wealthy classes of the Northeast and the Old South. For example, this 1875 illustration described this tavern scene as "a drawing of men drunk and sober dancing to rude music." *(Drawing from Edward King's* The Great South, *Hartford, Conn.: American Publishing Co, 1875, p. 176. University of Texas Institute of Texan Cultures at San Antonio.)*

lad narratives), which have served as an oral history of the Texas-Mexican border for over two hundred years. Representative of the *corrido* tradition, *El Corrido del Enganche*, tells the story of the Mexican workers who travel north to find opportunity:

> *La con está me despido*
> *con mi sombrero en las manos,*
> *y mis fieles companeros*
> *son trescientos Mejicanos.*

The German population that settled in the central region of Texas was best known for its *saengerfests*, public songfests organized on a statewide basis. The first *saengerfest* was held in New Braunfels in 1853. Organs and pianos were the main accompaniment for the German-American folk singers, but by the end of the century their European-inspired music was embellished by any instrument that could beat out a polka, from trumpets to the accordion. The Cajuns who had migrated into Southeast Texas from Louisiana had similar styles and instruments. Of course, they brought much of the New Orleans influence (French folk songs and dances and a jazz fiddle style) to Texas and passed that heritage on to both the Anglo folk performers and the black country bluesmen.

Other ethnic groups—Swedes, Czechs, Italians—each had their own enclave which embraced a certain tradition and folk heritage. Some remained ethnically pure and maintained a close relationship with their European ancestry, but most folk traditions began to merge and reflect the developing Texas society. For example, the Mexicans borrowed the accordion and the polka from the Germans and made it an integral part of the Norteño sound. Anglo dancing styles were modified by Mexican customs, such as the two-step counter-clockwise dance movements that came from the promenade of Mexican dancers around the plaza. The rhythm and percussion instrumentation (drums, tambourines, marimbas) that pounded out the beat of all Texas folk sounds came from the Afro-American heritage.

The largest body of Texas folk music came from the Anglo and black communities. The majority of Texas immigrants were Anglo-American, and they came primarily from the southern states of Arkansas, Tennessee, and Virginia. They introduced the southern string band (consisting of guitars, banjos, and fiddles), as well as the ballads and marching songs indigenous to England, Scotland, and Ireland. The first Anglo folk song written on Texas soil was reportedly *The Brazos Boat Song*, composed in 1831 by Mary Holley, a cousin of Stephen F. Austin. Many of the Anglo-Texan folk materials were adaptations from songs of other regions or ethnic groups. Examples include *Red River Valley*, the Texas version of the northeastern folk song *Bright Mohawk Valley*; *Bury Me Not on the Lone Prairie*, a paraphrase of the old sea shanty *Bury Me Not in the Deep, Deep Sea*; *On the Banks of the San Antonio*, an adaptation of the southern standard *Old Salt River*; and *The Eyes of Texas*, from the traditional *I've Been Working on the Railroad.*

The dominance of Anglo music spread as a result of the numerous singing societies and musical associations in every city and village of the state. Anglo-Texan music was even taught in the public schools as the "legitimate" and "patriotic" music of Texas. It often emphasized military events (such as the Battle of San Jacinto, the fall of the Alamo, or the Mexican and Civil wars), or it canonized the heroes of Texas Independence (Houston, Austin, Bowie, and Crockett).

The Anglos not only brought their southern musical traditions to Texas, but they also brought their slaves. The music of the Afro-Americans was the backbone of every form of American popular music, and the experience in Texas was no exception. Their folk music combined the strong African rhythmic beats with the instrumentation of the southern mountain sounds, primarily banjos and fiddles. The lyrics of black Texas folk songs displayed a few traces of African influence, but the messages of hardship and hope usually described experiences unique to the southern slave culture. The first Texas folk song to achieve national recognition as well as lasting popularity was originally written and sung by Texas slaves. *The Yellow Rose of Texas,* the classic Texas folk song of the nineteenth century, was a slave ballad inspired by Emily Morgan, the young black girl who supposedly distracted General Santa Anna at the Battle of San Jacinto.

Perhaps the folk song most closely associated in the national mind with Texas, *The Yellow Rose of Texas* was an American folk favorite for over a century. A commercial success in 1936 after its release in commemoration of the Texas Centennial, it resurfaced in the 1950s as a pop hit. The song itself has undergone an evolution throughout its long history. By the turn of the century its lyrics had been changed and all references to the color of that heroine of the Texas Revolution, Emily, the "yellow rose," were eliminated. A number of other folk songs of the black community were victims of a subtle racism, and they became hits in an anglicized form. All of Texas society sang such black folk songs as *Down on the Rolling Brazos, The Boll Weevil Song,* and *Seek and Ye Shall Find.*

By the end of the nineteenth century, there was a significant body of both original and borrowed folk material within Texas society. It was the popular music of the age, and it could be found in churches, minstrel shows, medicine shows, fair and carnival performances, singing societies, local bandstand concerts, schools, and nearly every Texan's home. It was during this period of industrial growth and technological advance that the most important event in the history of music occurred. In 1877 Thomas Edison invented a rudimentary phonograph, and after he perfected a wax cylinder model in 1888, a musical

The New Hope Baptist Church Choir and Band of Waco was typical of many black church choirs in Texas in their utilization of full instrumentation—cornets, trombones, fiddles, bass violin, and drums. *(University of Texas Institute of Texan Cultures at San Antonio.)*

Mariachi and Tex-Mex *conjunto* bands have been fixtures on the San Antonio riverwalk for over a century. (*Drawing by Peyton Cooper, courtesy Frank Phelps. University of Texas Institute of Texan Cultures at San Antonio.*)

Peter Berg of Fredericksburg proudly displays his handmade German pipe organ in this nineteenth-century photo. (*Kilman Studio, Fredericksburg. University of Texas Institute of Texan Cultures at San Antonio.*)

and *What Shall We Do with a Drunken Sailor*) were enormous hits in those first days of popular music, but he was probably best known for his adaptations of Texas folk songs. Guion added or rewrote lyrics and then devised completely new arrangements for such American classics as *Home on the Range*, *Turkey in the Straw*, and *Arkansas Traveler*. It was David Guion's version of *The Yellow Rose of Texas* that made it a nation-wide pop hit in the 1930s. In addition to a successful career in the folk and pop fields, Guion wrote numerous hymns and gospel songs based on religious music he discovered while studying the folk traditions of Mexican, Indian, and black Texans.

Yet, of all the Texas composers who appeared near the turn of the century, none rivaled the stature, the achievement, or the genius of a shy, lonely young man from Texarkana. If there was one individual responsible for linking the Texas folk heritage to the commercial popular music of the twentieth century, that person was the "Father of Ragtime," Scott Joplin. Born in 1868, just three years after his parents were freed from slavery, Joplin and his music led a musical renaissance from 1895 until the First World War. It was a renaissance not only in structure and style, but also in spirit. It laid the foundation for jazz, rhythm and blues, and rock 'n' roll. Although the public rediscovered Scott Joplin during the ragtime revival of the early 1970s, his credentials as one of America's premier composers and performers have never been questioned by the musical community.

A ragtime craze swept the country in the 1890s, and for the first time southern songs and style played a predomi-

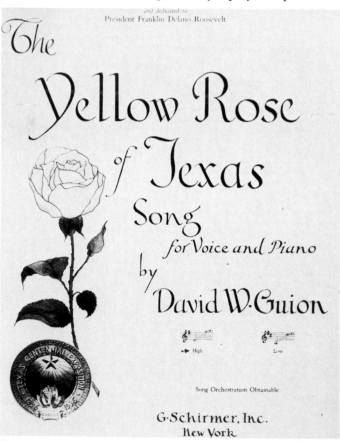

Sheet music for the popular Texas folk song *The Yellow Rose of Texas*. This 1936 arrangement by David Guion was dedicated to President Franklin D. Roosevelt and written in honor of the Texas Centennial. (*G. Schirmer, Inc., Texas Music Collection.*)

revolution had begun. As the recording business grew from a fledgling oddity to a prosperous industry, Texas composers began to have impact on a national scale. The first Texas songwriter to achieve national fame was Oscar Fox of San Antonio. Grandson of German immigrant Adolph Fuchs, a famous musician and classical-music teacher, Oscar Fox wrote hundreds of songs that emphasized Texas themes and drew on Texas folk traditions. He composed several original cowboy songs which stirred interest within New York publishing circles, and songs such as *The Hills of Home*, *The Rain and the River*, and *Corn Silks and Cotton Blossoms* did very well commercially.

Another major composer and arranger during the early years of commercial recording was David Guion of Ballinger. Guion's original works (*Ol' Paint, Ride Cowboy Ride*,

The Texas Panhandle's first band—the Mobeetie Brass Band. *(Courtesy of Margaret Schneider McIntyre. University of Texas Institute of Tex-* *an Cultures at San Antonio.)*

nant role in the cultural development of all regions of the United States. Ragtime created a new fascination with southern society and brought a new respectability to the music of black America. Musically, ragtime is defined as the syncopation of African rhythms in combination with the European system of tone and scale. The term originated from the concept of "playing in ragged time," or, in the words of an early ragtime composer, "tearing time apart." It was played on the piano and was characterized by one hand continually and gently beating out a percussive rhythm while the other hand played a syncopated melody. Ragtime was born in the cafes, saloons, brothels, and vaudeville shows of New Orleans, Memphis, St. Louis, and every black juke joint along the Mississippi River. Scott Joplin was not the first musician to play ragtime, nor did he give it its name, but he was the most important figure of the ragtime era and the one who transformed it from music bordering on respectability to America's favorite sound.

Scott Joplin learned to play the banjo, fiddle, and piano as a young boy in Texarkana, but his ability to earn a musical living and to write "rags" did not come until he left Texas for the Midwest. He struck commercial success in St. Louis and Sedalia, Missouri, with two of his most famous compositions, *The Entertainer* and *Maple Leaf Rag.* But as ragtime's appeal grew and became international in scope, the more established white composers received the praise and critical acclaim. In an effort to gain recognition as a serious songwriter, Joplin wrote a folk ballet (*Ragtime Dance*) and two operas (*A Guest of Honor* and *Treemonisha*). None of these were received favorably at the time, and along with a series of personal crises, their failure destroyed Scott Joplin's will and artistic drive. He died in 1917 from a degenerative mental capacity brought on by syphilis he had contracted some twenty years earlier. His friends claimed that his condition was aggravated by years of frustration and bitterness over the rejection of his music as serious work. The tragedy of Scott Joplin has no doubt been repeated thousands of times in our past. Here was a genius—a man whose gift enriched our lives—yet no one acknowledged his talent and contribution until he was gone.

The style and compositions of Scott Joplin dominated American popular music through the World War I years.

Sheet music to Scott Joplin's most successful composition, *The Entertainer. (Texas Music Collection.)*

Oscar Fox of San Antonio was the first Texas composer to receive worldwide recognition for his promotion of Texas and its culture. With Texas folk and cowboy songs New York publishing houses began to romanticize and exploit western and Texas themes. *(University of Texas Institute of Texan Cultures at San Antonio.)*

David Guion — one of Texas music's most prolific composers and arrangers. *(G. Schirmer, Inc., Texas Music Collection.)*

During that time another Texan, Euday Bowman, made his musical mark in the ragtime world along the Mississippi. His *Twelfth Street Rag* was one of ragtime's popular melodies. The acceptance of ragtime by American society in many ways opened the door for the development of jazz in the 1920s and the resulting experimentation in every aspect of American music. With the expanded sales of sheet music, cylinder records, and phonographs, it helped popularize music as an industry. But most importantly, ragtime introduced white America to the creative spirit of black America on a massive scale. American music, and American society, would never be the same.

The ragtime era was over by 1920, a pivotal year in the development of the music industry. Commercial radio broadcasts began that year, and within a decade one-half of all the homes in America would be tuned in. There was also an explosion in the sales and promotion of a new technology in the early twenties, disc records. The combination of these factors created a demand for more songs and more performers to satisfy the musical appetites of millions of Americans whose social lives centered around their radios and Victrolas. No state produced more composers and performers to meet those musical demands than Texas. Their diversity of folk traditions provided the impetus that moved nineteenth-century music into the twentieth-century world of big business, mass entertainment, and artistic expression.

♫

Lefty Frizzell—a legendary figure in the history of American country music. *(Courtesy of Leon and Chic Carter.)*

2
Early Country

Waltz across Texas with you in my arms

Waltz across Texas with you in my arms,
Waltz across Texas with you;
Like a storybook ending
I'm lost in your charms,
Waltz across Texas with you.

Waltz Across Texas
Ernest Tubb
Talmadge Tubb

The origins of country music are interwoven with the roots of the American people. Usually identified as southern folk music, the country sound originated with the rural, working-class people who immigrated to the United States during the seventeenth and eighteenth centuries. Those early settlers from England, Scotland, and Ireland not only developed political, economic, and religious institutions that dominated the New World, they also introduced a variety of folk songs and ballads that defined the style and substance of modern country music. As the Anglo-American pioneers moved westward across the sprawling frontier, folk music served as a means of retaining their European culture and traditions, but it also mirrored the new experiences unique to each ethnic group and each geographical region of America. That European heritage remained strongest and most consistent in the South — a southern musical legacy that during the 1920s became a commercial enterprise known as hillbilly, mountain, country-western, honky-tonk, or plain "country" music.

The historical and sociological development of Texas closely followed the model of other southern states, and the music of the Anglo-Texans was no exception. The South was settled by agricultural people who valued and perpetuated a rural lifestyle. Their society was an isolated one, and from that isolation emerged an atmosphere of conservatism and conformity. The musical tradition in the South, as well as Texas, was a stabilizing factor; it helped preserve and validate older values and reinforce ties to previous generations. In contrast, the folk music of the North was more diverse and constantly changing due to the influence of heavy immigration, an industrial economic base, and the growth of urban centers. The institution of slavery also accounted for the defensive and reactionary climate that led to the regional cohesiveness of the South and its failure to break from a self-imposed isolation. When southerners migrated across the Red and Sabine rivers in the 1820s, the songs they sang were the same ones that had been heard for two centuries on the tidewater of Virginia, in the back country of the Carolinas, and in the Appalachian valleys of Tennessee.

Country music in Texas had a number of identifiable characteristics. The most dominant style was the string band, a three-piece group that utilized the fiddle, banjo, and guitar. Variations from this format often included other instruments, such as the harmonica, bass, piano, hornpipes, or the dulcimer. The focus of the string band was usually a solo singer whose vocal range extended to a high, nasal pitch. Despite the adroit instrumentation of the performers, the song lyrics were the music's most distinct feature. The lyrics addressed an entire range of rural concerns: family ties, regional pride, hard economic times, and the evils of city life. The string bands performed at community dances, called hoedowns or breakdowns depending on the locale, and occassionally a string band played at church functions. Very few Texas musicians were full-time professionals before commercial recording began in the 1920s, but every village could point with pride to its own expert fiddler or guitar picker. Local competitions led to statewide contests among fiddlers, and in some cases the complete string ensemble participated for the honors. As a result of one of these "old fiddlers" contests, the first recordings of country music were made.

The distinction of being the first country music performer to record went to a Texan, Alexander Campbell (Eck) Robertson of Amarillo. Known for years throughout Texas as a champion fiddler, Robertson's expertise generated enormous publicity in 1922 when he traveled to the annual Confederate Veterans' Reunion in Richmond, Virginia. Robertson was billed as "the world's best breakdown fiddler," and his success at the Richmond contest led to a recording session in New York. Victor Records produced six fiddle tunes by Eck Robertson (and partner Henry Gilliland) at that historic 1922 session, the most famous being *Sallie Goodin*. Robertson had moderate success with three other songs during the decade (*Ragtime Annie*, *Turkey in the Straw*, and *Arkansas Traveler*). He continued to perform at dances, house parties, and on radio programs in and around the Texas Panhandle during the thirties and forties. The highlight of his musical career came in 1965 at the Newport Folk Festival when participants staged a tribute to Robertson for his role as country music's first recording artist.

Eck Robertson's pioneering effort was a boon for the Texas fiddle-band tradition. Fiddle bands became a full-fledged industry in January of 1923 when radio station WBAP in Fort Worth produced the nation's first "barn dance" show. The host of that initial broadcast was Captain M. J. Bonner, known as the "Texas Fiddler." The WBAP "Barn Dance" triggered an explosion of hillbilly radio programs all over the country, from the WLS "National Barn Dance" in Chicago to the WSM "Grand Ole Opry" in Nashville. Radio exposure enabled several Texas bands to gain national followings during country music's first decade as a commercial enterprise. From the Dallas area came the Solomon and Hughes Band, the Steeley and Graham Band, and the Dallas String Band. There was the Peacock Fiddle Band from Cleburne and the Shelton Brothers (Joe and Bob) from Rylie Springs. Many of the string bands that had their own radio shows (such as the East Texas Serenaders, Oscar and Doc Harper, and Prince Albert Hunt) began the transition from the older Texas fiddle tradition to the more innovative styles that appeared in the 1930s as western-swing. Another group utilizing the string-band format during the late twenties and early thirties was the Beverly Hillbillies, led by Texan Stuart Hamblen. The Hillbillies became national stars from their base in Los Angeles, but most of their material was Texas-oriented. Hamblen was nationally renowned as a composer and eventually directed his singing and songwriting abilities toward gospel music.

As Texans became prominent on a national scale, it was apparent that elements in their music were in contrast to

Country music in Texas was synonymous with southern folk music in both style and instrumentation. Note the variety of instruments pictured in this early Texas combo—banjo, guitar, fiddle, clarinet, mandolin, and dulcimer. *(Austin History Center, Austin Public Library.)*

Eck Robertson, the first country musician to make a recording, was the most renowned Texas fiddler in the 1920s. As a youth in Amarillo, Eck reportedly once fashioned a makeshift fiddle by skinning the family cat and stretching the skin over a gourd. *(John Edwards Foundation, UCLA.)*

the music of their southeastern cousins. There was such ethnic and geographical diversity in Texas that country music became more experimental and more exciting than the static and rigid hillbilly and mountain sounds emanating from other southern states. One of the major ethnic influences on this Texas style was the Norteño music that developed in South Texas and the northern states of Mexico. Stars from that genre included Narciso Martínez, Santiago Jiménez, and Lydia Mendoza. Their impact was felt far beyond the Hispanic community; it extended into the southern and central regions of Texas through country rhythms, instrumentation, and lyrics. Norteño music (often referred to as *conjunto*) blended traditional Mexican styles with the instruments of the German and Czech settlers who had moved into the northern Mexico mining communities at the turn of the century. The *conjunto* and the mariachi bands that flourished in El Paso and San Antonio attained little visibility outside their regions, but other Texas musicians, aware of their vitality and originality, embraced many of their sounds.

The German population exerted its cultural and social influence on Texas country music long after its early contact with the Mexicans. Settling primarily in the hill country of Central Texas, the German-Americans combined southern folk songs with their polkas and waltzes and expanded the range of the typical country dance band with the addition of the accordion. Carrying on the German and Slavic tradition in Texas from the 1930s to the present is Adolph Hofner of San Antonio. Hofner's long-lived career is symbolic of the German contribution to Texas music. His forte is versatility; his repertoire ranges from German polkas to Tex-Mex to western-swing.

Lydia Mendoza has promoted the Tex-Mex sound for over forty years from the Rio Grande Valley to California. She is the acknowledged "Queen of Norteño." *(Chris Strachwitz, Arhoolie Records.)*

Stuart Hamblen (far right) was the leader of the California-based Beverly Hillbillies. The Hillbillies promoted the Texas string-band style on radio programs and in several western movies. *(John Edwards Foundation, UCLA)*

Santiago Jiménez y sus Valedores—one of Texas' most popular *conjunto* bands. The accordion is the heart of the "conjunto" sound. (left to right: Ismael Gonzales, Santiago Jiménez, Manuel Gonzales). *(Courtesy of Santiago Jiménez. University of Texas Institute of Texan Cultures at San Antonio.)*

For half a century Adolph Hofner (third from left) has performed his unique blend of German and Tex-Mex folk music in San Antonio and throughout South Texas. *(Courtesy of Leon and Chic Carter.)*

Moon Mullican—"King of the Hillbilly Piano Players." Mullican is shown here performing over radio station WSM, the "Grand Ole Opry" in Nashville. *(Country Music Foundation.)*

The Cajun sounds of Louisiana and Southeast Texas were also strong contributors to the unique Texas style. The music of the bayou was dominated by hard-driving rhythms featuring energetic fiddlers and accordion players. Its development in the 1930s was popularized by figures such as Fiddlin' Harry Choates, the Hackberry Ramblers, and country-swing pianist Moon Mullican. The Cajun style, today often referred to as zydeco, is a vibrant combination of southeastern country and black rhythm and blues. The Cajun sound, along with the Mexican and German folk music heritage, was a concrete example of the growing complexities of Texas music and its movement to embrace all the diverse ethnic elements within Texas' borders.

Artistically, Texas country music was becoming a richer, more creative force in the social life of the 1920s and 1930s; it was also becoming big business. The first country record in music history to sell a million copies was *The Prisoner's Song*, with *The Wreck of the Old '97* on the flipside. That event catapulted country music into international prominence, and it made singer Vernon Dalhart country music's first commercially successful star. Born Marion Try Slaughter in 1883 on a ranch near Jefferson, Texas, Dalhart took his name from two Texas towns (Vernon in North Texas and Dalhart in the Panhandle) that he visited while working cattle as a teenager. Dalhart was originally a singer of popular songs and even appeared in several light operas as a tenor. When his career faltered in the early twenties, he persuaded Victor Records to let him record songs from his youth in rural Texas, songs disdained by most record executives as hillbilly. As a result, Dalhart virtually saved the troubled Victor and became one of the best-known recording artists in the country during the next decade. The song that insured Dalhart's fame as a country music star was his 1927 release of *Home on the Range*. His version of that Texas cowboy ballad was a hit in both the pop and country fields and was the record that helped launch the cowboy and Texas crazes that dominated movies and country music in the 1930s.

And yet, Vernon Dalhart's greatest contribution was the respectability he brought to country music. Having had formal musical training and exposure in the pop and classical worlds, Dalhart was responsible for helping to remove the stigma and negative imagery associated with country music outside the South. It took many more years and millions of dollars of profit before that lower-class hillbilly image was completely blurred, but Vernon Dalhart's pride in Texas and its native folk music began the process.

With the phenomenal popularity of Vernon Dalhart, country music was recognized as the leading form of entertainment in the South as the 1930s approached. Three dominant and distinct musical styles emerged during that decade of economic depression and social upheaval, and all three originated in Texas with Texas musicians achieving star status in each area. The singing cowboys and the western-swing bands are each of such importance that they will be discussed in following chapters. The third direction taken by the country sound in the 1930s was honky-tonk music. All three styles were interchangeable, of course, and a performer from Texas most likely considered himself or herself adept at moving from one to the other with ease.

The term *honky-tonk* came from the slang of southern blacks who referred to beer joints as "tonks." The description first appeared in a country song in 1936 when Al Dex-

Vernon Dalhart became country music's first superstar when his recording of *The Prisoner's Song* went gold in 1925. *(John Edwards Foundation, UCLA.)*

The career of Floyd Tillman has spanned five decades. His early stint with the Blue Ridge Playboys helped launch the Texas honky-tonk tradition. *(Brian N. Kanof.)*

Al Dexter—the original Texas honky-tonker. *(Country Music Foundation.)*

ter recorded *Honky-Tonk Blues.* Dexter, from Troup, Texas, was the most popular of the early honky-tonkers. His later hit, *Pistol Packin' Mama,* was the definitive honky-tonk song of the World War II era. These songs had a strong dance beat, but their lyrics accounted for their distinctiveness and popularity. This was post-Prohibition America, and the ever-increasing number of bars and taverns expanded the audience for an aspiring country singer. It was in this environment that Texas oil field workers, railroaders, truckdrivers, farmers, and ranchers all relieved their working-class frustrations and Depression-era fears. Every tavern from the rail yards of Dalhart to the refineries of Orange had either a live band or a jukebox belting out messages of love, divorce, cheatin', drinkin', and survivin'. In particular, it was the jukebox, introduced throughout the South in 1935, that spread the Texas honky-tonk sound to blue-collar America.

The first notable honky-tonk band of the 1930s was the Blue Ridge Playboys, playing out of Houston. The members of that group were a who's who of the Texas honky-tonk sound: lead singer and guitarist Floyd Tillman, steel guitarist Ted Daffan, fiddler Leon Selph, pianist Moon Mullican, vocalist and guitarist Chuck Keeshan, and guitarist Dickie McBride. The group was often labeled as a western-swing band, but its years on the Texas dance hall circuit were over-shadowed by the prolific honky-tonk songwriting of the individual members. Ted Daffan wrote classics like *Worried Mind, Headin' Down the Wrong Highway*, and *I'm a Fool for You*, but he is best known for one of America's most renowned pop and country songs, *Born to Lose*. Many a heartache found empathy as the jukebox delivered Daffan's lyrics of fate, "Born to lose, and now I'm losing you."

Ted Daffan was a master at blending the Hawaiian guitar style with the country steel. After leaving the Blue Ridge Playboys, he led his own group, Ted Daffan and the Texans. In 1939 he wrote *Truck Driver's Blues* — the first of an endless number of country truck-driving songs — and in doing so, he insured himself prominence as the originator of one of country music's most enduring traditions.

Aubrey "Moon" Mullican was probably the most versatile musician among the Blue Ridge Playboys. He was unquestionably honky-tonk's leading pianist, but his innovative style led him to Cajun music, blues, ragtime, jazz, and country-swing. Mullican's giant hit of 1950, *Jole Blon* (written by Fiddlin' Harry Choates), and one of his own compositions, *Cherokee Boogie*, placed him at the forefront of country music pianists and validated his billing as "King of the Hillbilly Piano Players."

The singer and songwriter most identified with the honky-tonk style is Floyd Tillman. He grew up in Post, Texas, and became a professional musician in 1933 when he joined Adolph Hofner's "country German" band in San Antonio. After becoming an original member of the Blue Ridge Playboys in 1935, Tillman was one of the first country per-

Jerry Jeff Walker and Ernest Tubb (right) at the Broken Spoke in Austin, 1980. *(Rick Henson.)*

Ernest Tubb — the "Texas Troubadour." *(John Edwards Foundation, UCLA.)*

Kenneth Threadgill has been a major force in the evolution of country music in Austin. While perpetuating traditional country styles with his versions of Jimmie Rodgers' yodels, his honky-tonk (Threadgill's) provided an outlet for younger musicians to experiment with variations of country-laced folk, blues, and rock. Threadgill is pictured here with his gold record from the Willie Nelson movie *Honeysuckle Rose*. *(Brian N. Kanof.)*

formers to use an electric guitar. But it was his West-Texas-drawl singing style and his songwriting ability that earned him national acclaim. Forty years after he helped inaugurate the honky-tonk sound, Floyd Tillman still has the magic, evidenced by his warmly received performances at Willie Nelson's Fourth of July picnics during the 1970s. His best-known compositions include *I Love You So Much It Hurts, It Makes No Difference Now*, and his song of infidelity that became standard fare for every jukebox, *Slippin' Around*. A common message of today's country songs, the honesty of *Slippin' Around* created enormous controversy when Tillman released it. A later Tillman effort, *She's Slip-*

pin' Around, attacked the hypocrisy of the double standard and began the tradition of the "answer song."

Another one of the legendary performers who bridged the musical generation-gap at Willie Nelson's picnics was Ernest Tubb, the Texas honky-tonker who brought the style to Nashville in the 1940s. Tubb took the Texas sound to the Grand Ole Opry in 1943, following the release of his first giant hit, *Walking the Floor over You*.

Ernest Tubb was born in 1914 on a three-hundred-acre cotton farm near Crisp, Texas. His mother was one-fourth Cherokee and played the piano and organ; it was her influence that shaped Ernest's early fascination

Bill Neely's country-folk sound reveals a blues influence that can be traced to his association with Jimmie Rodgers. *(Burton Wilson.)*

The Herrington Sisters—country-gospel stars from Wichita Falls. *(John Edwards Foundation, UCLA.)*

with music and poetry. There was another major influence in the teenage life of Ernest Tubb, and that was the industry-proclaimed "Father of Country Music," Jimmie Rodgers. Rodgers moved to Kerrville in 1929 (four years before his death) and became identified with Texas and its rich, developing country music tradition. Mrs. Jimmie Rodgers met Ernest Tubb in 1935, and knowing his devotion to Jimmie's music, she presented her husband's guitar to Tubb. Tubb's first few years as a performer were patterned in the same style and lyrical focus as that of the "Singing Brakeman," but his distinctive style slowly emerged during the late thirties as he wandered through Texas appearing on local radio programs and working at a variety of nonmusical jobs. He sang in the honky-tonks of San Antonio, Midland, San Angelo, and Corpus Christi, sometimes for as little as a dollar a night, sometimes as part of his job as a salesman for beer, flour, or mattresses.

Ernest Tubb paid his dues in those Texas dance halls and on those early-morning radio shows, and his adopted title, the "Texas Troubadour," could not be more appropriate in describing his forty-plus years on the road. With nearly three hundred performances a year and legions of devoted fans, Ernest Tubb has proven to be country music's most enduring personality. In testament to his contributions to country music, to other entertainers, and to the millions who love his music, Tubb was inducted into the Country Music Hall of Fame in 1965. The accolades continue to pour in, and although the advancing years have slowed his pace, Ernest Tubb is still on the road, still singing his unique brand of Texas honky-tonk.

Ernest Tubb was one of hundreds of performers whose inspiration came from the life and music of Jimmie Rodgers. Two other Texas singers who fall into that category and who are still performing are Bill Neely and Kenneth Threadgill. Jimmie Rodgers taught Neely his first guitar chord and helped him launch his half-century career as a country-folk-blues artist. Kenneth Threadgill, who often plays and yodels with Neely, also acknowledges his debt to Jimmie Rodgers. He has been yodeling Rodgers' songs from his landmark combination honky-tonk and gas station, Threadgill's, in Austin since 1933.

While Al Dexter, Floyd Tillman, and Ernest Tubb were honky-tonkin' across Texas, people in the South and Midwest were getting their daily dose of Texas music from a radio. The Depression severely crippled most American industry, but radio reached its peak of prosperity in the 1930s and 1940s. The dramatic growth of country music during this period was a direct result of the proliferation of country music programs on the hundreds of new radio stations. Texas stations promoting honky-tonk and western-swing included WACO in Waco, WFAA in Dallas, WOAI in San Antonio, KPRC in Houston, KGRS in Amarillo, KFJZ in Fort Worth, and with the highest-rated program in Texas, the "Big D Jamboree," KRLD in Dallas. All of these stations followed the same successful format as the first radio barndance program, WBAP's "Barn Dance" in Fort Worth.

Country-oriented radio programs were instrumental in selling everything from laxatives to Jesus, and therefore the performers were identified in the public's mind more with products than with music. The Crazy Water Crystals Company of Mineral Wells sponsored country music shows throughout Texas, promoting "hillbilly bands" along with their cure-all and fountain-of-youth miracle, Crazy Water Crystals. The magic crystals were nothing more than a lax-

America's greatest folksinger, Woody Guthrie. The message of Woody's music was as clear as the messages that he often inscribed on his guitars—"This machine kills fascists" and "This machine surrounds hate and destroys it." *(Courtesy of Okemah, Oklahoma, Public Library, Texas Music Collection.)*

ative. The flour companies also vied for the country music fan's dollar: Ernest Tubb for Gold Chain Flour and the Light Crust Doughboys for Burrus Mill. Dr. J. R. Brinkley, broadcasting to every corner of the United States and Canada over XERA in Ciudad Acuña across the Rio Grande from Del Rio, sold country music and—in one of American advertising's greatest challenges—transplants of goat glands to impotent males. Brinkley's medical license was revoked, but he became a wealthy man and a leading entrepreneur in country music.

Another profitable industry, radio evangelism, linked its image with the country music sound. It was a natural marriage; often the sermon and the lyrics were interchangeable. Evangelists interrupted the music at regular intervals and sold every product imaginable: prayer cloths with sequin lyrics, Bibles bound with the American flag, baby rabbits blessed by the local singing star, and autographed pictures of Jesus Christ. However, some very talented gospel groups did spring from the Texas evangelist network. The Stamps Quartet started on KRLD in Dallas and the Campbell Family emerged from Houston; from Lubbock came the Chuck Wagon Gang; the pride of Wichita Falls was the Herrington Sisters, Olga, Winnie, and Ida Nell. Mixing gospel with country, the Herrington Sisters became continental stars;

their programs were transmitted from Panama to Alaska via the Mexican border stations. The Texas gospel tradition grew following World War II, and many of the country stars expanded their material to include the demand for religious music. The most visible example of that trend was the career of Stuart Hamblen, who turned his country and cowboy songwriting ability to the gospel field in the early 1950s and scored his biggest hit, the pop spiritual *It Is No Secret What God Can Do.*

In many respects the radio rivaled religion for the devotion of Americans during the Depression. Rural Texas tuned in every day hoping to find some relief from deflated farm prices and the loss of topsoil blown to Arkansas. The Depression devastated the South economically, but it spawned a musical tradition that has had a profound effect on the political and social history of the United States. That tradition was the music of social activism, or as it was labeled twenty years later, "protest music." In reality, it was the purest form of American folk music — songs addressing the social injustice that destroys the spirit of individual women and men. The protest song is older than the Revolution of 1776, and it was natural that it should be reborn amidst the fear and frustration of the Depression years. The man most responsible for renewed interest in social consciousness via the folk song was a young Oklahoma drifter who spent the Depression decade in Texas. He was America's greatest folk singer, Woodrow Wilson Guthrie.

Woody Guthrie left Oklahoma in 1926 at the age of fourteen and hoboed through Texas. He traveled among the oil camp workers of the Gulf Coast and eventually joined other members of his family in the Panhandle town of Pampa. Woody spent ten years in the Texas Panhandle — an experience that molded his preoccupation with the dispossessed, the worker, the farmer, and those who valued people over profit. He worked at a variety of jobs during those dust bowl years, but he played at country dances whenever possible and was even a member of the Pampa Junior Chamber of Commerce Band. Woody often reminisced about the Panhandle, "where the wheat grows and the oil flows, where the dust blows and the farmer owes." His *Blowin' Down That Old Dusty Road* brings that sentiment to life.

After leaving Texas, Woody became the champion of the migrant-labor movement in California. His hundreds of folk and labor songs rank among America's most moving and inspiring messages. Often attacked for his vocal compassion for people of all colors and economic classes, Woody Guthrie was a genuine patriot — his patriotism embraced all of humanity. His body of folk songs is a library of American classics, such songs as *Roll On, Columbia, Oklahoma Hills, So Long It's Been Good to Know You, This Train Is Bound for Glory,* and his most famous, *This Land Is Your Land.*

Woody Guthrie once defined his own songwriting philosophy and his view of the role of music. His words hit

Woody Guthrie (far left) and the Pampa, Texas, Junior Chamber of Commerce Band in 1936. *(Courtesy of Okemah, Oklahoma, Public Library, Texas Music Collection.)*

at the heart of the power and importance of music to American society, and they describe the tradition and spirit of Texas music.

> I hate a song that makes you think that you're not any good. I hate a song that makes you think you are just born to lose. No good to nobody. No good for nothing. Because you are either too old or too young or too fat or too thin or too ugly or too this or too that. Songs that run you down or songs that poke fun at you on account of your bad luck or your hard traveling. I am out to fight those kinds of songs to my very last breath of air and my last drop of blood.
>
> I am out to sing songs that will prove to you that this is your world and that if it has hit you pretty hard and knocked you for a dozen loops, no matter how hard it's run you down and rolled over you, no matter what color, what size you are, how you are built, I am out to sing the songs that make you take pride in yourself and in your work. And the songs I sing are made up for the most part by all sorts of folks just about like you.

Woody did not achieve widespread commercial success in his lifetime, but he did become a cult figure in New York folk circles during his tenure as a member of the Almanac Singers. More than any social critic or political figure, Woody Guthrie brought the Depression-era message of rural America to urban ears. Despite personal attacks against him and his music during the McCarthy witch hunt and a debilitating nerve disease that eventually took his life, Woody was the dominant force in spurring the folk music revival of the 1960s. And more importantly, the life and music of Woody Guthrie awakened a social awareness and concern in a new generation of Americans.

While Woody spent the post–World War II years pickin' in the cabarets of Greenwich Village, Texas society and Texas country music underwent dramatic change. The slow rural exodus that had begun some twenty-five years earlier increased to a rapid pace, and the resulting social changes had a profound impact on musical tastes and trends. As more Texans moved to the city, there was a corresponding decline in the popularity of the singing cowboys and the western-swing bands. On a national level, there was a growth of interest in the southeastern sound, culminating with the dominance of Nashville in the country music industry. But while other Texas styles were struggling, the honky-tonkers continued to prosper as the South became a more urban and industrialized society. It was in this post-war era that a number of transplanted Texans in Nashville helped propel Texas honky-tonk to the top of the country charts.

The jukebox king of the late 1940s and early 1950s was one of the true legendary figures in country music history, William Orville Frizzell of Corsicana. Nicknamed Lefty from his days as a boxer, Frizzell scored major hits with *I Love You a Thousand Ways* and *If You've Got the Money, I've Got the Time*. It was Lefty's voice that affected millions of followers—a rich, tenor drawl filled with intense emotion.

Goldie Hill was the major female country performer from Texas in the early 1950s. (*Doug Hanners Collection.*)

One of Frizzell's accomplishments, four songs in the top ten simultaneously, has never been equaled. After experiencing a number of career and personal problems following his initial success, he rebounded in the early sixties with two more enormous country hits, *The Long Black Veil* and *Saginaw, Michigan*. Frizzell re-emerged in the seventies as a songwriter before his unexpected death from a stroke in 1975. The countless honors, testimonials, and songs dedicated to his memory are evidence of the debt owed to Lefty Frizzell by performers and writers in the country music world.

There were other artists in the 1950s who kept the Texas sound at the forefront of country music. Charlie Walker, a disc jockey out of San Antonio, had a major hit with *Pick Me Up on Your Way Down*. Jimmy Heap, along with his Melody Masters, received national attention with *Release Me* and *The Wild Side of Life*. Hank Thompson and the Brazos Valley Boys were consistently on the country charts as well as being one of the most popular dance bands in the Southwest. In the Panhandle, Honest Jess Williams promoted country music with both live performances and two decades of exposure on radio and television. One of the most popular media personalities in the Austin area, Arleigh Duff, wrote such country classics as *Y'all Come* and *It's the Little Things*. Leon Payne, blind since childhood and a one-time Playboy with Bob Wills, emerged as one of Texas' finest songwriters of the era with *Lost Highway* and *I Love You Because*. Slim Willet was a singer and composer of the pop hit *Don't Let the Stars Get in Your*

Johnny Horton—country music's leading proponent of the saga song. *(Country Music Foundation.)*

The songs of Jim Reeves still get such consistent airplay on country radio stations that many of his fans do not realize he died in 1964. In addition to his tremendous commercial success, the unique Reeves style of country-pop justified his 1967 selection to the Country Music Hall of Fame. *(Mrs. Jimmy Heap.)*

Eyes. Goldie Hill scored hits with *I Let the Stars Get in My Eyes* and *Say Big Boy.* A headline performer on the "Louisiana Hayride" radio program out of Shreveport, Hill retired following her marriage to Tennessee star Carl Smith. Another veteran of the "Louisiana Hayride" was Johnny Horton of Tyler. Horton moved from Texas honky-tonk roots to become the acknowledged leader of the historical song style.

The saga folk songs by Johnny Horton in the late 1950s were examples of country music's first commercially successful crossover hits. Country in style and instrumentation, Horton's records did extremely well on the pop and rock charts. They included *North to Alaska, The Battle of New Orleans, Johnny Reb,* and *Sink the Bismarck.* By 1960 Horton was appearing on the "Grand Ole Opry" and playing to sold-out houses nationwide. Despite his identification with the saga song, he was from the Texas honky-tonk school, one of his own compositions being *I'm a Honky-Tonk Man.* Horton's spectacular rise to stardom ended with a fatal automobile accident in November of 1960 following a performance at the Skyline Club in Austin.

As Nashville grew more dominant in the late fifties, country music performers rejected the honky-tonk style and the rural instrumentation that had become their trademark. The fiddle virtually disappeared; the steel guitar became a rarity; orchestras and background choruses overshadowed the solo singing style. The slicker, diluted country sound was Nashville's response to the more successful pop and the rapidly growing rock industry. One of the leading country

performers to benefit from that change was Jim Reeves. Reeves was from the same East Texas county (Panola) as singing cowboy star Tex Ritter, and he would later join his fellow Texan in the Country Music Hall of Fame. The career of Jim Reeves got its initial boost when he landed a spot on the "Louisiana Hayride," and that led to his first hit record, *Mexicali Joe.* Reeves' voice was too smooth and resonant to fit the honky-tonk image, so he helped lead the new Nashville emphasis on more commercial, popular music presentations. Before his death in an airplane crash in 1964, Reeves recorded two of the most successful songs to come out of Nashville in the 1960s, *He'll Have to Go* and *Four Walls.*

Another Texan in Nashville well known for his low-key, heavily orchestrated sound was Ray Price of Perryville. Price began his career as a honky-tonker in the tradition of Ernest Tubb and Hank Williams. The Ray Price of the 1950s was perhaps Texas' most versatile entertainer. His individualistic style embraced western-swing, the country blues, a mellow country-pop sound, and his staple, hard honky-tonk. In the late sixties Price had a pronounced image change, and his music moved toward a smoother pop sound. The peak of his commercial success came after his recording of Kris Kristofferson's *For the Good Times.* Price and his band, the Cherokee Cowboys, are responsible for several of Nashville's best-selling records of the last twenty years: *Heartaches by the Number, City Lights, Night Life,* and *Burning Memories.*

21

Ray Price performing at a 1980 taping of "Austin City Limits." *(Photo by Scott Newton, courtesy of "Austin City Limits.")*

Ray Price—during his honky-tonk days in the late 1950s. Note Price's bass player on his left, Willie Nelson. *(Leon and Chic Carter.)*

Duffy's Mountaineers combined traditional southeastern country music with the Texas sounds of the 1940s and 1950s. *(Courtesy of Leon and Chic Carter.)*

Country music faced turbulent change and threatening challenges as the 1960s began and rock 'n' roll continued to grow. Many predicted the decline, or even the death of the southern and rural dominated sounds. At best, critics saw country music surviving as an isolated, regional variation of popular or rock music. But the critics failed to understand that country music was a legitimate art form within the spectrum of American music. It would no more disappear than the thousands of folk songs that have documented our history for three and a half centuries; country music is twentieth-century folk music for a large proportion of American society.

As for commercial success and media exposure, there were factors developing on the Texas horizon that would lead country music to unparalleled prominence in the sixties and seventies. There were revivals ahead in honky-tonk and western-swing; there were innovations ahead in country-rock and the Austin sound. The music was becoming more complex, more diverse, wider in scope and substance. At the forefront of the resurgence of country music—those whose talent and spirit defined the new directions—were the Texans.

♫

Carl Sprague—the first singing cowboy. *(Country Music Foundation.)*

3

The Singing Cowboys

I'm back in the saddle again

I'm back in the saddle again
Out where a friend is a friend,
Where the longhorn caddle feed
On the lowly jimson weed,
I'm back in the saddle again.

Back in the Saddle Again
Gene Autry
Ray Whitley

No legend or myth in American history is as enduring and romantic as that of the cowboy. His popular image—riding the range and winning the West atop a sturdy, dependable mount, his white hat fighting off the twin Texas foes of wind and sun—is symbolic of the American dream. He is a noble, somewhat lonely figure who embodies qualities sacred to the American past: freedom, individualism, sacrifice, commitment to completing a job that must be done. The cowboy is one of the few American institutions whose reputation and appeal have remained unscathed by the social and economic changes of the twentieth century. That legend began in Texas, and it was promoted and nurtured by the Texas folk music of the cowboy era.

Great herds of longhorn cattle roamed Texas during the years of the Texas Republic and preceding the Civil War. Originally brought to Texas by the Spanish and worked for generations by Mexican *vaqueros,* these cattle became Texas' most immediate source of wealth following the Civil War. With no railroad network yet in operation, entrepreneurs on the Texas frontier rounded up the longhorns and drove them up the trail to the railheads at Dodge City, Abilene, or Sedalia. The music of these drovers served two purposes. First, there was a need to round up strays and soothe them at night. These were the "dogie songs," ballads or rhythmic

yells sung directly to an audience of seven-hundred-pound beeves. Second, the music served as entertainment—attempts to relieve the boredom that accompanied a journey across the monotonous Texas plains. The songs told of the work, land, and cattle. They also told of the play—the euphoria at the end of the trail when a paycheck was spent for the necessities of the cowboy's existence: a game of five card stud, a bottle of Kentucky whiskey, the feel and smell of a Kansas dance hall girl.

A number of factors helped transform the reality of the cowboy, a regionally isolated man of the nineteenth-century working class, into a symbol of the American experience on the western frontier. Dime novels glorified the adventure and romance of the West, and Wild West shows deified the Indian fighters and buffalo hunters. But the folk songs of the cowboy had the greatest impact in perpetuating his legend. The man most responsible for collecting and promoting those original cowboy songs was John A. Lomax, Texas folklorist and ballad hunter. With his publication of *Cowboy Songs and Other Frontier Ballads* in 1910, Lomax preserved the lyrics and melodies of 112 cowboy tunes whose authors and origins were anonymous. The Lomax anthology spurred an academic interest in western folk music and generated commercial potential with the general public.

Lomax went directly to the cowboys and ranch hands and recorded the history and sounds of the American West: *Home on the Range, The Streets of Laredo, The Old Chisholm Trail, Bury Me Not on the Lone Prairie*, and the most popular of the early cowboy songs, *Git Along Little Dogies.*

> **As I was a-walkin' one morning**
> **for pleasure,**
> **I spied a cow puncher a-ridin'**
> **along.**
> **His hat was thrown back and his**
> **spurs was a-jinglin',**
> **And as he approached me was**
> **singin' this song.**
> **Whoopee ti yi, git along, little**
> **dogies;**
> **It's my misfortune and none of your**
> **own.**
> **Whoopee ti yi, git along, little**
> **dogies;**
> **For you know Wyoming will be your**
> **new home.**

John Lomax was two years old in 1869 when his family piled into a covered wagon and left Mississippi. They settled in the cedar-covered hills of Bosque County, Texas, just a few miles from the Chisholm Trail. Lomax grew up listening to the cowpunchers sing along the trail and around the campfire. He began collecting the lyrics of these original American folk songs as a teenager, and he was determined that they be preserved and treated seriously as genuine social history. As a student at the University of Texas, Lomax attempted to present his collection of cowboy songs as "frontier literature." He was ridiculed and told that the music was "tawdry, cheap, and unworthy." Ten years later, at Harvard, he received the encouragement and financial assistance that finally enabled him to publish the folk songs of the Texas cattle drives. John Lomax devoted a half century to the music of Texas, and he had the foresight, understanding, and compassion to see beyond race, wealth, status, and preconceived concepts about that music. His work in a variety of areas of Texas folklore, from cowboy songs to the country blues of black Texans, helped define the future of Texas music and all the diversity it encompassed.

Despite the invaluable work of John Lomax, the cowboy was losing his appeal as society became more urban and industrialized. It was not until the early 1930s, the beginning of the Great Depression, that the image of the cowboy was resurrected and placed at the forefront of America's heroic figures. In times of crisis and confusion, America looks backward for its answers and its heroes, backward to a less troubling, less complex era. Those answers and those heroes America found in the cowboy legend. People sought refuge from the economic and social chaos of the thirties by escaping to the local theater, and there was the cowboy — riding into the sunset, kissing his horse, and singing a love song to both his favorite girl and his restless herd.

There is general agreement that the merging of movies with music in the 1930s gave impetus to the popularity of the cowboy as a historical figure. However, a number of

John A. Lomax—"The Ballad Hunter". *(Barker Texas History Center, University of Texas at Austin.)*

Songs of the Cow Puncher

A Lecture by

Prof. John A. Lomax

Of The University of Texas

Describing the growth and development of the cowboy songs and frontier ballads, with examples of the verses. An account of the wild life on the trail where these ballads had their origin. A breath of the breezy West of yesterday, from which the poetry and romance of the frontier is rapidly passing.

AUDITORIUM, ENGINEERING BUILDING

Thursday Evening, Dec. 8, 1910, 8 O'clock

ADMISSION - - - - FREE

The Faculty, students and public generally are cordially invited to be present

The pioneering work of John Lomax brought an academic respectability to the study of the cowboy and his folklore. This 1910 poster promoting a Lomax lecture, open to both the public and university students, is an example of his attempts to reunite Texans with their folk heritage. *(Barker Texas History Center, University of Texas at Austin.)*

The guitar and the fiddle were as important to the cowboy during his leisure hours as his horse and branding-iron were from sunrise to sunset. Since half of the cowboys in Texas were either black or of Mexican descent, the cattle range provided an ethnic interaction that helped create a sharing of musical tradition and social custom. *(SMS Ranch, Stamford, Texas. University of Texas Institute of Texan Cultures at San Antonio.)*

Texas country singers began recording western music in the 1920s, and they justly deserve the title of the "original singing cowboys." The first cowboy song to be recorded was Carl Sprague's 1925 release, *When the Work's All Done This Fall.* Sprague grew up on a ranch between Alvin and Houston and was one of the few cowboy singers who had actually worked and lived as a cowboy. He made twenty-eight recordings with Victor Records in New York, and it was his early success that encouraged Victor to record an entire catalog of cowboy singers. Sprague's renditions of the Texas folk songs *Bury Me Not on the Lone Prairie* and *Cowboy Love Song* created a rush by other performers to record the cowboy ballads of the nineteenth century, many of which could be found in John Lomax's collection. Carl Sprague never pursued a commercial career after his recording sessions with Victor, but he occasionally performed publicly and had a weekly radio program at Texas A&M University. If any one performer can lay claim to being the first singing cowboy of the recording era, it is Carl Sprague.

A contemporary of Carl Sprague, and also a real cowboy, was Jules Verne Allen from Waxahachie. Allen had a large following on radio stations throughout the Southwest during the late 1920s and early 1930s. He performed regularly on WOAI in San Antonio and billed himself as "Longhorn Luke." Allen, who had worked as a cowboy on ranches in Texas and Montana since the age of ten, was a true western folk singer. His material reflected the music of the trail drives, the roundups, and the rodeos, a topic that steadily gained the attention of urban audiences as the events spread from the West to the cities of the East. As was the case with most of the early singing cowboys, Jules Verne Allen also depended on the traditional Texas ballads collected by John Lomax as the major source of his repertoire.

Meanwhile, other Texas singers were discovering their nineteenth-century folk roots, performers such as Texas Jim Robertson, the Cartwright Brothers, Marc Williams, and Goebel Reeves, also known as the "Texas Drifter." Reeves not only sang cowboy songs, he introduced the world of the drifter, a new theme in the rapidly expanding field of country and western music. Goebel Reeves lived the life of a hobo, a drifter who rode the rails with a guitar and harmonica. Although he came from a middle-class family in Sherman, Reeves rejected money, security, and even musical acclaim. Many of his original songs, such as *Hobo's Lullaby* and *The Cowboy's Prayer,* are now considered country classics. His version of *Big Rock Candy Mountain* brought him national recognition, and he subsequently performed on radio programs from New York to Nashville. Reeves' style was characterized by the authenticity of his lyrics and his high-pitched yodel. In fact, he often boasted that the most satisfying aspect of his career was teaching Jimmie Rodgers how to yodel. Goebel Reeves was an original—the first of the country singers to sing of the frustration and the freedom of "goin' on the road."

Even though the trail-blazing efforts of Sprague, Allen, and Reeves met with success, widespread appeal of the cowboy sound was limited to the Southwest. Not until he was discovered by Hollywood did the singing cowboy win national acceptance. That occurred in 1930 when Texan Ken Maynard sang four original cowboy songs in the film, *Songs of the Saddle.* Maynard starred in a number of "horse operas" during the early thirties; their plots usually revolved around the title song, such as *The Strawberry Roan* or *In Old Santa Fe.* Action was the important ingredient in Maynard films, and, except for supplying a title or plot line, the music was of secondary value. Maynard's songs were momentary respites between chase scenes or bar room brawls, and he never sang more than two or three songs per film. It proved to be a successful formula for the infant Hollywood film industry. Maynard's blend of western action with western music was Hollywood's major revenue source from 1930 to

Ken Maynard was the first actor to sing in a western movie, *Songs of the Saddle*, in 1930. (*John Edwards Foundation, UCLA.*)

1935. However, most film biographers refer to Ken Maynard as an actor, not a singer. That designation was reversed in the case of a protégé of Maynard, the most famous of all the singing cowboys, Gene Autry.

Gene Autry was born in 1907 on a small tenant farm near Tioga, Texas. His father was a horse and cattle trader, but the major influence on Gene Autry's early life was not the romantic environment of a Texas ranch, it was the music that surrounded Gene Autry as he grew up in the Red River Valley. His mother, Elnora, encouraged Autry's obvious musical talents and taught him to play the guitar. That guitar accompanied Gene and his mother as they routinely sang the gospel songs he had learned at nearby Indian Creek Baptist Church, pastored by Autry's grandfather. Autry's first professional music job, with the Fields Brothers Marvelous Medicine Show, came after his family had moved to Oklahoma. And yet, he never seriously considered music as a career until a coincidental meeting with America's foremost humorist of that era, Will Rogers. Autry was working as a railroad telegrapher near Chelsea, Oklahoma, when Rogers came in to send a telegram. Seeing a guitar lying at Autry's side, Rogers made several song requests. Impressed by the soft, tenor voice, Rogers encouraged Autry to turn professional and try New York. Within a year, Gene Autry recorded his first song on Victor Records.

A recording contract did not mean immediate success in New York, so Autry returned to Oklahoma and performed on his own radio program on KVOO in Tulsa. The following year he moved on to the WLS "Barn Dance" in Chicago where he was billed as "Oklahoma's Singing Cowboy," although most of the songs in his repertoire were not cowboy songs but southern folk tunes in the hillbilly tradition. Nevertheless, his Texas heritage and his self-proclaimed admiration for the music of Jimmie Rodgers led to a continual identification of Autry as "western." Gradually, he began to shift his style to fit the image. In 1934 Autry took his image and his guitar to Hollywood, and the transformation of the small-town Texas singer to America's number one movie hero had begun.

Gene Autry had a loyal audience in rural America before his movie career began to flourish. In 1931 he co-wrote and sang one of country music's biggest hits, *That Silver Haired*

Daddy of Mine. But the large urban audiences, and especially the Hollywood producers, were not familiar with him or his music, and therefore he was considered a financial risk by the major studios. Finally he landed a movie role in the Ken Maynard film *In Old Santa Fe.* Autry had a small singing part in the movie, but the response from the public was so great that Republic Studios rapidly increased his exposure. Following another appearance with Maynard in *Mystery Mountain*, Autry starred in a twelve-part serial called *The Phantom Empire.* He played himself in that 1934 science-fiction western, setting a precedent for the rest of his career. In 1935 Autry made his first feature film, *Tumbling Tumbleweeds.* The title song was also a nationwide success and began a string of combination film and record hits, such as *Mexicali Rose* and *South of the Border.* For the next decade and a half Autry's box office receipts and record sales validated his billing as the "Nation's Number One Singing Cowboy."

True to his Texas heritage, Autry continually utilized Mexican themes as a source for his music and movies. Romantic adventures along the Texas or California borders were the backbone of Gene Autry films, and ballads and waltzes from south of the border were a trademark of his music. Some of his greatest hits included *El Rancho Grande, It Happened in Old Monterey, My Adobe Hacienda,* and *Vaya Con Dios.* His recordings were often large-scale productions employing the Big Band sound of the thirties, complete with horns, fiddles, accordions, and castanets. While many Americans were neglecting the rich Spanish tradition in the Southwest, the music of Gene Autry constantly reminded America that the cowboy and the cattle industry were Mexican in origin.

The impact of Gene Autry's phenomenal success was felt in other segments of the entertainment industry. Cowboy and western themes gained "credibility," meaning they made enormous amounts of money. Autry brought his cowboy

Gene Autry was well known as a pop singer before his movie career began in 1934. (*John Edwards Foundation, UCLA.*)

During the 1930s, radio stations all over the country featured live cowboy singers on their daily programing. *(Courtesy Bill Corkery.* *University of Texas Institute of Texan Cultures at San Antonio.)*

adventures to radio with his CBS program, "Melody Ranch," and he helped pioneer television production. His Flying A Productions dominated the western-oriented programing on the fledgling television industry of the early 1950s. The formula followed in Autry's movies and his music was a simple one; he always wore the white hat; he always triumphed over evil. He exposed corruption and protected the weak and poor. The just and the good-hearted always won in the end. It was the perfect plot for a country seized by fear of the Depression and the tyranny of facism in Europe. It was a fantasy world that gave hope to a beleaguered generation. But the story of Autry's life is much more exhilarating and inspiring than his B westerns and his cowboy songs. He is living proof of Middle America's version of the American dream, a rural North Texas farmboy grown into a multi-millionaire financier.

The first of the singing cowboys to gain acceptance and artistic recognition from New York entertainment circles was Woodward Maurice "Tex" Ritter. Born in Panola County's East Texas pine forests, Tex Ritter rivaled Gene Autry as the leading western film and recording star of the 1930s. Ritter's interest in the American West and his love of the cowboy legend flowered while he was a student at the University of Texas. There he studied with the foremost authorities on the cowboy and his music: the noted folklorist J. Frank Dobie, cowboy-song composer Oscar Fox, and the ballad hunter himself, John Lomax. Ritter attended Northwestern Law School for a year, but he returned to Texas in 1929 to take a singing job on KPRC radio in Houston. After touring the South with a western musical show, Ritter decided to try New York. He was literally an overnight success, thanks to his Texas drawl and his reputation as a "real" cowboy. He landed a major role in the Broadway production *Green Grow the Lilacs* (the play that provided the

Gene and Champ performing on the CBS radio program, "Gene Autry's Melody Ranch." *(John Edwards Foundation, UCLA.)*

Tex Ritter was at the height of his musical and movie career when this publicity photo was signed in 1939. The handwritten message on the picture was a personal note to Ritter's friend John Lomax. *(Barker Texas History Center, University of Texas at Austin.)*

framework for the musical *Oklahoma*), and he also performed on several New York radio programs. It was chic in the New York social world to tune in to one of Tex Ritter's radio roundups. From 1932 to 1936 he hosted such shows as "Tex Ritter's Campfire," "The WHN Radio Barn Dance," "Cowboy Tom's Round Up," and WOR's "The Lone Star Rangers."

In 1936, at the peak of his popularity in New York, Tex Ritter moved to Hollywood. During the next twelve years Ritter appeared in seventy-eight films and recorded hundreds of songs. His first record, *Jingle, Jangle, Jingle*, written by Texas songwriter Cindy Walker, began a string of hits that spanned two decades. Among those were *Good-bye Old Paint*, *Have I Stayed Away Too Long?*, *High Noon*, and his largest commercial success, *Hillbilly Heaven*. As Ritter's film career diminished in the late forties, he expanded his singing style to include more country and pop material. He remained a nationally visible personality in the fifties by hosting a California-based radio barn dance, the "Town Hall Party." In 1964 Tex Ritter was inducted into the Country Music Hall of Fame, an organization that he helped found.

N o performer was more responsible than Tex Ritter for bringing the term *western* into the musical world. His fame in New York brought a new respectability to country music, and that resulted in the removal of the derogatory connotations surrounding "hillbilly" music. No longer was a country singer promoted as a southern country bumpkin; he was now a westerner, a cowboy who had hero status in American folklore. It was all imagery, of course. The western garb and the fake cowboy names had little to do with the music, but Hollywood and the recording companies seized the opportunity to ride the success of Autry and Ritter. There is no doubt that the entertainment industry destroyed the purity of the cowboy heritage and commercialized a genuine folk song tradition. But perhaps the end result of the innumerable fake, rhinestone cowboys was a positive one, a plus for the country music industry as a whole. For the cowboy and the music that romanticized him had become an international phenomenon, and the entire spectrum of American music benefited from this new alliance between the hillbilly and western sounds.

There was a period during the late 1930s when it was considered a handicap in the country music business if you were not a Texan. Many singing groups, to capitalize on the Texas craze, implied that they had just ridden in from the bunkhouse. It was assumed that the California-based Sons of the Pioneers were Texans, but actually only two of them, Hugh and Karl Farr, were Texas-born. One member of that ensemble later emerged as the last of the great movie and singing cowboys, Leonard Slye, alias Roy Rogers. Although Rogers was often identified as being Texan in origin, in truth he was from Ohio. However, his wife Dale Evans, a singing and movie star in her own right, was from Uvalde and author of their theme song, *Happy Trails To You*. In a similar vein of false imagery, Gene Autry's backup band was widely perceived as Texan. But the only native Texan in the Cass County Boys was Fred Martin. There was an endless array of performers named "Tex" or "Cowboy" who had never seen the Texas prairie, but their musical contribution was consistent with the Texas tradition of blending the sounds of the rural South and West.

As more and more Texas bands and performers of the thir-

T. Texas Tyler was one of Nashville's biggest stars in the late 1940s. He was primarily a traditional country singer, but his Texas heritage encouraged his publicists and record label to promote him as a singing cowboy. *(John Edwards Foundation, UCLA.)*

of jazz and blues integration with country music, was viewed by much of the public as a singing cowboy—most likely a result of the cowboy movies he and his western-swing band appeared in during the early 1940s.

For the two decades between Ken Maynard's first western musical film and the rise of television in the 1950s, the singing cowboy reigned supreme in the world of country music. A number of Texas country performers took advantage of and perpetuated the cowboy tradition in appearance, name, and musical style. Tex Owens had a succession of hits, topped by the enormously popular *Cattle Call*, (later to become a crossover pop hit by Eddie Arnold). The sister of Tex Owens, Texas Ruby, was one of the more famous "singing cowgirls." Louise Massey, another of the cowgirls, achieved success as a singer and composer with hits like *In My Adobe Hacienda*. And the Girls of the Golden West (the Good Sisters) gained a national reputation after leaving West Texas. There was also Cowboy Slim Rinehart, the radio cowboy whose shows were broadcast out of the Mexican border stations. Monte Hale was a singing cowboy who received his greatest recognition as an actor. T. Texas Tyler was a singing cowboy star of the late forties, but his major hits on the country charts had no relation or reference to the West or cowboy life. Two of his compositions, *Deck of Cards* and *Remember Me*, have been recorded by a wide variety of popular artists. He later followed the pattern of another Texas country-cowboy singer, Stuart Hamblen, and devoted his career to gospel material.

ties and forties began to experiment in a variety of musical directions, the distinction between what was cowboy, country, or western-swing was obscured. For example, Bill Boyd and His Cowboy Ramblers did capitalize on their Texas origins and the resulting cowboy image, but their musical skills extended beyond country into jazz and pop numbers. They were a dance band, and two of their most successful releases, *Under the Double Eagle* and *Lone Star Rag*, were jazz-oriented fiddle tunes. Much of their music defied identification with the cowboy experience, and the cowboy image was in many ways a restrictive label. Similarly, Bob Wills, a genius

One of the most popular Texas groups of the forties was Foy Willing's Riders of the Purple Sage. Foy Willing left Texas as a young man and landed a job as a pop music vocalist on a New York radio station. After relocating in California in 1940, he joined forces with two other Texans, the Dean brothers (Eddie and Jimmie). The Riders of the Purple Sage found success after they appeared in several Roy Rogers' films and had a major hit with *Ghost Riders in the Sky*. Their western-oriented lyrics were overshadowed by dramatic harmonies, a sound copied by many of the groups coming out of Hollywood in the forties and early fifties. The Dean brothers had already achieved moderate success before joining the Riders of the Purple Sage. They were regulars on the "National Barn Dance" in Chicago and were best known as composers of country songs. Eddie Dean wrote two of country music's classics,

Texas Ruby Owens appearing on the Curly Fox radio program. *(Texas Music Collection.)*

Eddie Dean (center, with guitar) was one of Hollywood's successful composers during the singing-cowboy era. He also performed in several westerns during the 1940s, as in this scene from the movie *Black Hills. (John Edwards Foundation, UCLA.)*

Hillbilly Heaven and *One Has My Name, the Other Has My Heart.* While living in Hollywood, the Dean brothers wrote for the movie studios as well. Of all the Texas songwriters, however, Cindy Walker probably had the greatest proficiency as a contract writer for the Hollywood film companies. She scored big hits with *Leona, Bubbles in My Beer, Dusty Skies,* and *Warm Red Wine.*

One of the few original singing cowboys still performing is Red River Dave McEnery. His early fame originated with the New York audiences who were intrigued with his colorful, if not bizarre, saga songs. Red River Dave had roles in several cowboy movies during the 1930s and was one of the first singing cowboys to have his own radio program. His early hits, such as *Amelia Earhart's Last Flight,* have been updated to include *The Ballad of Patty Hearst* and a somewhat irreverent song dedicated to the Ayatollah in Iran. Red River Dave's narrative ballad style is reminiscent of the Mexican *corridos,* which he no doubt borrowed from the balladeers in his native San Antonio.

A significant consequence of the tremendous commercial success of the singing cowboys on record and on film was the development of a viable recording industry in California. After Gene Autry's pop-novelty song *Rudolph the Red-Nosed Reindeer* sold over nine million copies, the industry leaders realized the crossover from country-western to pop was a profitable leap. The California-based branches of

Capitol Records and Columbia Records took the lead in utilizing the nationwide appeal of the cowboy performers and their material. Pop recording stars scored some of their greatest hits with western-oriented Texas songs; for example, the Bing Crosby version of Bob Wills' *New San Antonio Rose,* Mitch Miller's rendition of the Texas folk song *The Yellow Rose of Texas,* and Rosemary Clooney's hit of *This Old House* by Stuart Hamblen. The 1950s was the decade when pop music discovered country, and it had been the Texans who made it happen.

By the mid-fifties television had all but destroyed the commercial appeal of the musical westerns. As the singing cowboys moved from the Silver Screen to riding herd on Saturday morning TV adventures, the reality of the nineteenth-century Texas trail hand and his music was further obscured. Cowboy music was now reduced to a thirty-minute vehicle promoting the sponsor's cereal or toothpaste. Country singers from Nashville to New York dressed in exaggerated costumes that would make a real cowboy cringe with embarrassment. America had completely distorted its most majestic hero by petty commercial exploitation. Those simple, yet inspiring, cowboy folk songs uncovered by John Lomax and the Texas folk music that comprised the backbone of the western sound in the thirties and forties had disappeared. In the words of a latter-day singing cowboy, the first Texas Jewish country star Kinky Friedman, the "faded, jaded, fallen

The Girls of the Golden West (Dolly and Millie Good) were from Muleshoe, Texas. Their harmonies and yodels made them one of country music's most popular acts. *(Texas Music Collection.)*

Ann Jones and her Western Sweethearts—singing cowgirls from Houston. *(Doug Hanners Collection.)*

Red River Dave McEnery was the first country music performer to appear on a television broadcast (1939). Here Red River Dave performs at the 1981 Kerrville Folk Festival. *(Brian N. Kanof.)*

cowboy star" had been "sold American."

And yet, despite dramatic change the cowboy and his music have survived serious assault by both commercialization and neglect. Whenever it appears that the cowboy will fade from American culture, there is a resurgence of Texas chic to revive him. And even though the cosmic cowboys in Austin and the urban cowboys in Houston now ride barstools instead of cutting horses, the cowboy lives on in the lyrics of today's folk and country music. None of those endless verses is a greater tribute to the spirit of the West than a 1969 song by Texas singer-songwriter Steven Fromholz. In *The Man with the Big Hat* Fromholz combines the ballad style of a nineteenth century Texas folk song with the finest in frontier poetry.

> *I can tell you stories 'bout the*
> *   Indians on the plains.*
> *Talk about Wells Fargo and the*
> *   comin' of the trains.*
> *Talk about the slaughter of the*
> *   buffalo that roamed.*
> *Tell of all the settlers come out*
> *   lookin' for a home.*
>
> *I've seen a day so hot your pony*
> *   could not stand*
> *And if your water bag was dry don't*
> *   count upon the land.*
> *And winters, I've seen winters when*
> *   your boots froze in the snow*

> *And your only thought was leavin'*
> *   but you had no place to go.*
>
> *I rode the cattle drives from here to*
> *   San Antone.*
> *Ten days in the saddle and weary to*
> *   the bone.*
> *I've rode from here to Wichita with-*
> *   out a woman's smile*
> *And the fire where I cooked my*
> *   beans was the only light for miles.*
>
> *Now the high lines chase the*
> *   highways and the fences*
> *   close the range*
> *And to see a workin' cowboy is a*
> *   sight that's mighty strange.*
> *A cowboy's life was lonely and his*
> *   lot was not the best.*
> *But if it wasn't for the life he lived*
> *   there wouldn't be no West.*

The Old Chisholm Trail is now paved over by Highway 281, but the legacy of the cowboy and his role in American history remains—the innocent simplicity of rural life, the dignity of the working man and woman, and the nobility of the land and those who respect it.

♫

Mance Lipscomb — the last of the Texas country bluesmen. *(Chris Strachwitz, Arhoolie Records.)*

4

The Country Blues

See that my grave is kept clean

There's one kind favor I ask of you,
One kind favor I ask of you,
Lord, there's one kind favor I ask
of you,
Please see that my grave is kept clean.
See That My Grave Is Kept Clean
Blind Lemon Jefferson

The blues began in 1619 when the first African slave stepped onto the Virginia shore. Throughout the next three hundred years a musical, social, and cultural tradition evolved in the American southland that emerged as the most unique and distinctive sound of the twentieth century. African musical styles, dominated by elaborate rhythmic structures and a heavily accented beat, were eventually "Americanized" by the experiences of black men and women in the southern slave culture. Those experiences were chronicled by generations of musical expression and served as an oral history documenting the oppression and brutality of America's most tragic institution. The blues were the emotional and spiritual outlet that became a source of strength for those who had no power, of pride for those who had no identity, and of hope for those who had no future.

While Texas may have been part of the western frontier for many, it was genuinely southern for the black Texans who worked the cotton patches and cane fields. The slaves who first came to East Texas in the 1820s brought with them the Afro-American musical heritage indigenous to the other states of the cotton kingdom. They brought their songs: the field hollers, work chants, ritual shouts, chain gang moans, and gospel rhythms. They brought their instruments: the banjos, panpipes, mouth organs, recorders, three-string guitars, and any cylindrical object to serve as a drum. For the next century the so-called race music in Texas existed in a state of incubation waiting to give birth to ragtime, jazz, and rock 'n' roll. With the exception of the Mississippi Delta region, no geographical locale was as rich a spawning ground for the country blues and all its derivative musical styles as was Texas.

The blues became a recognizable and acceptable element in the chaotic and diffused world of American popular music following the First World War. Commercial recording ventures were just beginning, and the producers from the major race labels (black records), particularly Columbia Records and Paramount Records, converged on Texas and the Mississippi Delta to find the "real," the "original" bluesmen. There were a great many blues artists already in the flourishing musical centers of the Midwest, from Chicago through St. Louis to New Orleans. But the record companies rejected the performers they considered urban imitators and searched for the innovators, the men and women at the heart and soul of the country blues. They found them in the bottomlands of the Brazos and the scorching pine forests to the east. They found Texans—inspired, talented, and determined.

The early Texas blues artists were influenced in four spe-

37

cific areas that emanated from their southern musical heritage. The first, and most likely the dominant area of influence, was the Negro spiritual that had developed through generations of slavery. These gospel ballads reflected more than religious concerns; they addressed the whole range of human emotions and relationships. The language of the spirituals was highly figurative and intensely personal, with a religious orientation more reminiscent of Eastern philosophies than of Southern Baptist fundamentalism. The second major influence on the Texas blues tradition was the occupational experience of southern blacks. An overwhelming majority were agricultural workers, and the sharecroppers' repertoire of work chants was just as valuable as pick sacks or strong backs. Although no longer legally bound to the fields by slavery, the black Texan's economic plight was still one of poverty and futility. Work songs, consisting of a variety of syncopated hollers and shouts, provided a release from the physical demands and tedious boredom of the fields. No doubt they also created an emotional bond among those who shared the similar frustrations of the tenant-farm system. In addition to the spiritual and the work song, prison experiences were a third theme among the country bluesmen. The chain gangs on the various Texas prison farms were the source of endless verses proclaiming the despair of prison life and the hope that soon it might end. The prison farms at Sugarland, Brazoria, and Sandy Point were training grounds for an education in the blues. The juke joints, brothels, and barrelhouses that stretched from the Red River to the Gulf were the fourth arena that contributed to the development of a unique Texas blues style. It mattered little if the musical performance was in the Third Ward of Houston, the red-light district of Galveston, or Deep Elm (pronounced "Ellum") in the northern section of downtown Dallas, bluesmen found the opportunity to break the oppression that had tied them to the Texas soil.

The most commercially successful of the country blues singers, as well as the very first to record, was a blind, 250-pound minstrel from the rolling farmland of Central Texas, Blind Lemon Jefferson. From 1925 until 1929, Lemon Jefferson released more than eighty recordings for Chicago-based Paramount Records and two for OKeh Records in Atlanta. The body of work accumulated in his brief recording career ranged from dynamic field hollers to sensitive prison ballads to moving spirituals. Blind Lemon Jefferson's songs had a beautiful lyrical quality delivered in a haunting style that justifiably signified him America's first great legend of the country blues.

Born in 1897 on a farm just a few miles east of Wortham, Lemon Jefferson lived a typical rural Texas childhood. His days were spent roaming mesquite-filled creek bottoms with eight older brothers and sisters. By nightfall the humidity of Central Texas had slowed the pace, and Lemon was often seen on the veranda curled around the family dog or perched in a live oak tree half asleep. Had it not been for the fact that Lemon was born blind, he probably would have lived and died on the sun-scarred farm of his youth. With no sight, no skill, no education, and certainly no hope, the "gift in his fingers" was Lemon's only possible salvation. He was fifteen years old when he took his guitar and voice to the streets of Wortham and nearby Mexia. Throughout his teen years Lemon gained a well-deserved reputation and a fairly loyal following in the black communities as an itinerant performer at church picnics and farm parties. As his fame and

Blind Lemon Jefferson—the first country bluesman to record. This 1928 promotion picture is the only known photograph of Jefferson. (*Texas Music Collection.*)

talent grew, so did his confidence; it was time to take the country blues to the city.

Lemon was twenty when he took his earthy, unpolished act to Dallas. The world of saloons, cafes, and brothels in north Dallas' Deep Ellum district was an intimidating and frightening experience for the young farm boy, but as a source for the blues it was unparalleled.

> ***Baby, times is so hard I almost call
>   it tough,***
> ***Baby, times is so hard I almost call
>   it tough,***
> ***I can't earn money to buy no bread
>   and you know I can't buy my
>   snuff.***
> ***My gal's a housemaid and she earns
>   a dollar a week,***
> ***My gal's a housemaid and she earns
>   a dollar a week,***
> ***I'm so hungry on payday you know
>   I can't hardly speak.***

Blind Lemon's *Tin Cup Blues* revealed the struggles inherent in an urban environment in a very graphic manner. Those early days in Dallas were chaotic for the blind, unknown performer, and in order to survive the hard reality of the city Lemon grudgingly accepted work as a professional wrestler. But singing jobs soon became more available, and by 1918 Blind Lemon was a regular in the bars and bawdyhouses of upper Elm Street, not only surviving but prospering. He bought a car, hired a chauffeur, and took his songs of rural poverty and urban alienation to the cities of the South and Midwest. The scope of Lemon Jefferson's

Blind Willie Johnson was one of the first gospel-blues singers to record. His thirty gospel recordings for Columbia sold exceptionally well and helped promote Blind Willie's unique "Hawaiian guitar style." (*Texas Music Collection.*)

music was mirrored by the diversity of his performances, from a tent revival in Waco to a medicine show in Mississippi to recording studios in Chicago.

Despite his extensive traveling and the variety of his audiences, Lemon seemed most comfortable in the red-light districts. His songs often included lyrics emphasizing his preference for southern women and southern liquor, and the consequences of overindulging in both. His blues contained vivid sexual images, some very obvious, as in *Mean Jumper Blues,* and some more subtle, as in *That Black Snake Moan.* Ironically, Jefferson frequently followed a song filled with sexual innuendo with a highly personal, intensely introspective spiritual. His most famous spiritual, *See That My Grave Is Kept Clean,* was recorded by Bob Dylan on his first album in 1961. The liner notes on that album describe the "surging power and tragedy of Blind Lemon Jefferson's blues." Those same notes claimed that the poignancy and passion of this simple song were in the finest tradition of the country blues. Dylan, future king of folk-rock and poet for the social activism of the 1960s, was also described as part of that same tradition begun so eloquently by Blind Lemon. And indeed, while listening to Lemon Jefferson's 1920s recordings, it is difficult not to hear traces of a young Bob Dylan some forty years later. The distance from the bottomlands of Central Texas to the folk clubs of Greenwich Village and from the country blues to rock 'n' roll is a short one.

The legacy left by Blind Lemon Jefferson to the world of American popular music is one of indisputable greatness and artistic impact, as evident from his many imitators in the twenties all the way to his namesake rock group of the sixties, Jefferson Airplane (later known as Jefferson Starship). The circumstances surrounding his death—he was found frozen to death in a Chicago snowdrift in 1929—only compounded the legendary quality of his music and the distressing tragedy of his short life. The emotion-filled moans from his vocal delivery and the shrieking whine of his guitar symbolized the desperation and hopelessness of black Texans trapped in the economic tyranny of racist America. Everything the blues symbolized for future generations was reality for the country bluesmen and blueswomen of the twenties and thirties, and once the style gained commercial respectability it proliferated from the streets and soil of Texas.

Most of the Texas blues singers followed the conventional blues format, a twelve-bar structure with three-line verses. The first and second lines of the verse were usually the same, and the last line was an answer or plea in response. A standardized, harmonic framework often identified the performer as to his or her geographical origins, but the message of most blues singers was strikingly similar. Blues poetry dealt with basic human emotions and experiences: love, death, sex, religion, and poverty. Rarely did blues artists address the sociological, or especially, the political factors that affected their images of the human condition. The blues were, and still are, an emotional and personal experience for both performer and listener. Those who seek a scholarly definition of the blues have missed the first step in understanding its beauty and power. The blues cannot be defined; they can only be felt.

Following World War I the rural exodus in Texas sent thousands of young men and women to the cities of Dallas and Houston. There the country blues were refined and began their shift toward the sophisticated, urban sound that led to the jazz and Big-Band era. Dallas was the hottest spot on the early blues circuit, and it boasted a number of clubs and theaters where new talent as well as established performers could work. Among the hundreds of juke joints and barrelhouses in the Deep Ellum district and throughout East Dallas were the Lincoln Theater, Ma's Place, 400 Club, Silver Slipper, Abe and Pappy Club, The Brown Derby, White's Road House, and countless others. Houston had its share of musical outlets also, such as the Rainbow Theater, Eldorado Club, and the Bronze Peacock. Even though Houston would emerge as the major blues center in the late forties and the fifties, for the aspiring blues artist Dallas was the place to be in the early decades. It was in the musically charged environment of downtown Dallas that the legacy of Lemon Jefferson endured and prospered.

There is little evidence by which to document this dynamic era in Texas musical and social history. The historians of the period were white, and they considered topics like music or black culture as of no academic value. Most information from the country blues era came from the musicians themselves or the recording companies that combed the Dallas area in the twenties and thirties. Columbia Records put an enormous amount of money and effort into tapping the Texas blues resources. They recorded bluesmen Perry Dixon, Coley Jones, Billiken Johnson, and Bobby Cadillac, all living in or near Dallas. One of Columbia's most successful recording artists was Blind Willie Johnson, from Marlin in Central Texas. His thirty gospel-blues records sold exceptionally well during the Depression years. Columbia also had the distinction of recording Whistlin' Alex Moore in 1929. Moore was the most famous blues pianist in Texas and the entire Midwest, and his combination of ragtime and blues had a great impact on later jazz and boogie-woogie styles. He was the first in a line of superb blues pianists who continued the "barrelhouse piano" tradition. Included in that group are Frank Ridge, Amos Milburn, R. L. McNeer, Big Boy Knox, Leon Calhoun, Harold Holiday, and Robert Shaw. Shaw, who now lives in Austin, is probably the last of the original barrelhouse pianists still performing, and he may well be the finest of them all. Dave Alexander, known as "Black Ivory King," is also an exponent of the Texas boogie piano style and is active in the San Francisco area.

Paramount, OKeh, and Vocalion were the other major record labels to enter the Texas blues market. OKeh recorded Little Hat Jones, Victoria Spivey, and Alger "Texas" Alexander. Following its success with Blind Lemon Jefferson, Paramount released a number of Texas blues songs by Willard "Ramblin'" Thomas and Johnny Head. Among Vocalion Records' success stories was that of Henry Thomas, usually billed as "Ragtime Texas." Thomas was undoubtedly one of Texas' more unique performers. He was a *songster*, a term that implied singing skills that encompassed a wide variety of styles and a diversity of song topics. Ragtime Texas was as comfortable in a brothel singing the blues as he was singing at a community picnic or church social. In addition to his high piercing vocals and wide range of lyrical subjects, Thomas was the first bluesman to record using quills, a set of graduated tubes more commonly known as panpipes. Born in 1874 near Big Sandy, Ragtime Texas was older than most of the country-blues singers, and his simple songster approach reflected a genuine folk sound that could only have evolved from someone one generation removed from slavery.

"Whistlin' " Alex Moore combined the piano styles of the ragtime era with the developing blues sounds of the 1920s and 1930s. *(Chris Strachwitz, Arhoolie Records. Courtesy of* Living Blues *magazine.)*

Huddie "Leadbelly" Ledbetter—"King of the Twelve-String Guitar Players of the World." *(Paramount Pictures, courtesy of* Living Blues *magazine.)*

Leadbelly and his wife, Martha. *(Texas Music Collection.)*

Robert "Fud" Shaw is the last of the Depression-era "barrelhouse pianists." The barrelhouse blues style was a jazz-oriented piano tradition that originated in the saloons of the South and the Midwest during the Prohibition years (stacks of barrels often lined one or more of the club's walls). *(Brian N. Kanof.)*

"Black Ace" (Babe Kyro Turner)—a proponent of the knife-and-bottleneck guitar style. *(Chris Strachwitz, Arhoolie Records. Courtesy of* Living Blues *magazine.)*

The man who most visibly represented the folk tradition of black Texans, and in a sense all of black America, was Huddie Ledbetter, more affectionately known by his millions of devotees as "Leadbelly." Leadbelly was many things to many people: a blues minstrel of extraordinary talent; a violent yet sensitive man full of contradiction; a man of great creativity but plagued by self-destruction; a folk hero who lived the emotional highs and lows of his music. Huddie Ledbetter was born in a two-room cabin on the Texas-Louisiana border near Caddo Lake and reared by his farm-poor father and his half-Cherokee mother. His father, Wes, and his uncle Terrell Ledbetter were both musicians, and they taught young Huddie a variety of musical skills as well as how to survive the roadhouses from Shreveport to Mar-

shall. Leadbelly was never an exceptional instrumentalist, but what he lacked in dexterity he compensated for in versatility. By the time he was fifteen he could play the guitar, piano, harmonica, mandolin, and the windjammer (a Cajun accordion). The powerful, bellowing voice and a subtle ability to lyrically capture the devotion of an entire nation propelled Leadbelly onto the national scene in the 1930s. But for all the success and adulation, Leadbelly's life was as tragic as the blues that consumed his existence.

During his teen years Leadbelly toured the club and dance circuit in and around the Leigh, Texas, and Mooringsport, Louisiana, region. There is evidence that he performed as far west as Fort Worth and eastward to New Orleans until he met Blind Lemon Jefferson in Dallas. They often performed together on the street corners of Deep Ellum and they shared the billing on one of their rare steady jobs at the Big Four Club. Their most profitable venture was a two-week run at the Mahogany Mansion, "a sporting house of the finest reputation" in Marshall. Leadbelly's self-proclaimed billing as "King of the Twelve-String Guitar Players of the World" had become a reality by 1916, if only in his musical kingdom of Northeast Texas.

Unfortunately, the fame of Huddie Ledbetter as an entertainer was often exceeded by his reputation as a man of great physical strength and violent temper. When that temper exploded, and that happened quite frequently in the dimly lit, drunken atmosphere of a Texas honky-tonk, Leadbelly could be found singing his country-blues from behind bars. He was sentenced in 1917 to a year of hard labor on the Harrison County chain gang for assaulting a woman. Over the next twenty-year period Leadbelly served three other prison terms, two for assault and one for murder. Ironically, it was his notoriety as an ex-convict that garnered him such acknowledgment and attention in the folk centers of New York. Twice he was paroled because two governors— Pat Neff of Texas in 1925 and Oscar Allen of Louisiana in

1934 — were impressed by his musical skills and the sincerity of his plea that he was merely a victim of circumstance. Concerning that contention, there was a good deal of controversy, due to the obvious fact that Leadbelly did have a penchant for bar room brawls. However, there is also evidence that his physical size and widespread reputation encouraged others to challenge him.

Many of Leadbelly's songs contained lyrics reflecting the desperation of life and spirit in the Texas penal system, an institution of brutal inhumanity and political corruption; its imprint on Leadbelly's music would never fade. One of his most famous songs, *The Midnight Special*, told of a superstition that had long been part of the prison farm folklore at Sugarland. If the engine light of the Southern Pacific Railroad happened to shine on an inmate at midnight, he could expect a rapid parole. The song was most likely co-written by Leadbelly and John Lomax, Texas' premier folklorist of the era, with the aid of Lomax's son, Alan. *The Midnight Special* has endured as Leadbelly's most identifiable legacy and it has been recorded by every generation in an amazing number of styles, from rock to country.

If you ever go to Houston,
Boy, you better walk right,
Well, you better not squabble,
And you better not fight.
Bason and Brock will arrest you,
Payton and Boone will take you
*   down;*
The judge will sentence you,
And you Sugarland bound.

Let the midnight special
Shine its light on me;
Let the midnight special
Shine a ever-lovin' light on me.

With the aid of John and Alan Lomax, Leadbelly received critical acclaim in New York, and the high-society crowd regarded him as a folk hero. He frequently worked with Woody Guthrie and other folk performers in Greenwich Village. But Leadbelly was a man of the country, and he repeatedly journeyed home to Texas and Louisiana, apparently to find some tranquillity and contentment in his life. From most accounts he never found it. He died a pauper in 1949 in a New York hospital with his wife, Martha, at his side.

The reputation of the Texas bluesmen was well entrenched by the 1930s, due primarily to the contributions of Lemon Jefferson and Leadbelly. For the most part, however, the Texas style was static and void of variation from the standard blues format. Compared to the Mississippi Delta songsters, the Texans depended more on personality than musical skill and experimentation. There were some exceptions, among them the knife-and-bottleneck guitar style. The use of a knife or a glass bottle as a slide over the neck of a heavy-necked steel guitar was very closely related to the steel guitar tradition of country artists and western-swing performers. Blind Willie Johnson was the leading proponent of knife-guitar compositions. His gospel songs were an eerie combination of his deep, gravelly voice accompanied by the

wails and twangs of his Hawaiian-sounding melodies. Two other bluesmen using similar techniques were Oscar Woods and Babe Kyro Turner, also known as "The Lone Wolf" and "Black Ace." They often played together at dances along the Texas-Louisiana border and had a radio program on a Fort Worth station. Their sound displayed the close relationship between the developing black blues forms and the Texas country styles.

As in all segments of American society, the opportunities for female performers in the twenties and thirties were limited. Women in the black communities of Texas were especially restricted in their freedom of personal and professional choices. The family, the church, and societal pressures portrayed the life of an entertainer as a sinful, degrading occupation that led to the evil depths of cafe society. This was ironic, since the female blues artists learned their musical skills in the church and continued to draw upon this religious heritage throughout their careers. The women, more so than their male counterparts, came from urban environments. Sexist restrictions and attitudes, as well as the harsh economic and social reality of the rural areas, effec-

Victoria Spivey and Bob Dylan at a 1961 recording session. *(Spivey Records, Texas Music Collection.)*

tively kept the women "down on the farm." But the powerful vocals and sensitive interpretations of the blueswomen from the cities provided quality, if not quantity, and their contributions proved to be invaluable and integral facets of the Texas blues tradition.

Victoria Spivey was the most famous and successful of this small but influential group of Texas women. She was born in a tenement house on Houston's east side in 1906 and grew up playing in the family string band headed by her father, Grant Spivey. Victoria became proficient at the piano, organ, and ukulele before she was twelve. During her teen years she played and sang in the Houston area and joined a local group, Lazy Daddy's Fillmore Blues Band. As the band's lead singer, Victoria led them to Dallas where the club and recording opportunities were greater. There she met and performed with Blind Lemon Jefferson. Before her twentieth birthday Victoria was renowned as the leading female blues singer on the Texas blues network from Galveston to Dallas. Her sisters, Addie and Elton, frequently performed with her after she began a series of national tours on the vaudeville circuit. The credits of Victoria Spivey read like a playbill of America's blues and jazz legends. She worked with Louis Armstrong and Bill "Mr. Bojangles" Robinson; she sang in numerous concerts at Carnegie Hall; she wrote hundreds of songs, one being the most recorded blues number of the 1920s, *Black Snake Blues*; she owned her own jazz and blues recording company and publishing house; and she was

Sippie Wallace — one of the early blueswomen from the Houston area — in a 1980 photograph. (*Bert Lek, Courtesy of* Living Blues *magazine.*)

regarded by her audiences, both American and European, as a legitimate heir to the title bestowed on her by publicity billing, "Queen of the Blues."

There were other women who played a prominent role in the emerging Texas blues phenomenon. From Houston came Sippie Wallace and her niece Hociel Thomas. There were Maggie Jones from Hillsboro and Monette Moore from Gainesville. Gertrude Perkins had a large following in the Dallas area. Earlier, there had been the ragtime blues sound of Lillian Glenn. All of these artists were classic blues singers, and their impact was felt far beyond the Texas border. After achieving local success, most of them joined touring bands and usually found themselves in Chicago, the major blues booking and publishing center. Following the jazz and rhythm and blues explosion of the 1940s, the exodus of women performers to the large recording studios of New York and the theatrical houses of Los Angeles accelerated. The women blues singers left Texas for the same reason the male performers left the Texas farms: to gain artistic acceptance and to seek economic opportunity.

One of America's legendary blues singers was an exception to this trend; Willie Mae "Big Mama" Thornton migrated to Texas in the 1940s. Originally from Alabama, Big Mama Thornton worked the clubs in Houston and began her recording career with producer Don Robey's Peacock label. Her success and popularity peaked at the time the world of American popular music discovered black rhythm and blues. Shortly after her rendition of *Hound Dog*, Elvis Presley made it a national hit and forever removed the distinction between "black" and "white" music. Fifteen years later, Texas' most famous disciple of blues and rock, Janis Joplin, record-

Willie Mae "Big Mama" Thornton was one of the most successful blues recording artists in the 1940s and 1950s. She bridged the gap between the southern country blues tradition and the post-World War II emergence of urban rhythm and blues. This photo was taken in 1969 at the Vulcan Gas Company in Austin. (*Burton Wilson.*)

ed Big Mama Thornton's composition *Ball and Chain.* There was more than symbolism present in this obvious musical relationship between the blues generation and the rock generation. Perhaps the blues were felt more intensely by the women, who had to face more obstacles in their struggle for acceptance and access. They brought a compassion and an emotional dimension to the blues that a man could not produce.

Blueswomen like Victoria Spivey and Big Mama Thornton broke new ground for women entertainers in urban Texas. Their commercial success opened the doors of the recording studios for a multitude of modern day women performers, beginning with the post war rhythm and blues and rock era. No longer were the women blues and jazz artists restricted to fronting dance bands; the audiences in Dallas, Houston, and San Antonio began to accept them as serious musicians and also to reward them financially. The musical home base of Spivey and Thornton was Houston, and as new record labels appeared there in the late forties (particularly Duke Records and Peacock Records), Houston surpassed Dallas as the center of Texas blues activity. Joining the prominent blueswomen in Houston was Texas' most dominant and most famous bluesman of the last thirty-five years, Sam "Lightnin'" Hopkins. More than any performer, Lightnin' made Houston the home of the Texas blues.

While Blind Lemon Jefferson was moanin' the blues on the dust-blown streets of Wortham, another Texas bluesman was being born forty miles to the southeast. Described by Chris Strachwitz of Arhoolie Records as "the most creative folk poet of our time—the King of the Blues," Sam Hopkins came from Centerville, an east-central Texas village in the middle of cotton country. Sam was playing a homemade cigar-box guitar by the age of eight, and his experiences as a teenage musician parallel those of Blind Lemon and Leadbelly. Much of his early exposure to the world of Texas music came from his older cousin Alger "Texas" Alexander. Alexander was one of the few Texas blues singers who played no instrument, so he often recruited Sam to accompany him at local picnics or on the streets of Houston. Texas Alexander was credited by such bluesmen as Smokey Hogg and Melvin "Li'l Son" Jackson as their inspiration to perform the songs of their youth and take pride in their black heritage. "Texas" was one of the last links between the old slave field holler tradition and the modern blues. He had a coarse, raspy voice, but one filled with a melodic quality that was rare in the country blues style. "Texas" had a modest recording career and continued to play with his cousin Sam until his death in the early fifties.

Despite the fact that Sam Hopkins continually performed his blues at dances, picnics, and family gatherings, he was in his mid-thirties before he attempted to earn a living as a musician. The Depression had hit the Hopkins family extremely hard, and the idea of going on the road to pick and sing the blues was a remote one for a man concerned with survival. However, after World War II Sam and his wife moved to Houston's south side, and he teamed up with a piano player named Thunder Smith. From that association came his nickname, Lightnin', and it has remained his trademark. Those first few years in Houston were very financially rewarding for Lightnin'; his recordings for Gold Star Records and Aladdin Records brought him both money and fame. His lifestyle devoured the money, but his talent increased the fame. The commer-

Lightnin'—the premier blues performer in Houston for four decades. *(Chris Strachwitz, Arhoolie Records.)*

cial success of Lightnin' was unrivaled by any of the country bluesmen except for the giants of the Mississippi Delta, Muddy Waters and John Lee Hooker. But no matter how many records he sold, Lightnin' always lived one step away from security. More than one pawnshop owner on Houston's Dowling Street holds a claim ticket for a Lightnin' Hopkins guitar.

Lightnin' was well known for his unique ability to improvise original material. That improvisation extended from his choice of lyrics to his masterful guitar techniques. But most of his own songs reflect his Depression era mentality, a legacy from which he was never able to escape. A few of the titles of his hundreds of compositions reveal his vision of the black man in American society: *Grievin' Blues, Unsuccessful Blues, The World's in a Tangle, Can't Be Successful Blues,* and *I Heard My Children Cryin'.* Mack McCormick, noted authority on the Houston music scene, paid this tribute to Lightnin' on the liner notes of an album he recorded for Tradition:

> He is—in the finest sense of the word—a minstrel: a street-singing, improvising songmaker born to the vast tradition of the blues. His only understanding of music is that it be as personal as a hushed conversation.

Lightnin' Hopkins dominated the Houston blues scene until his death in 1982. He was a country blues singer in the city, and he helped innovate the urban sound that has become an integral part of the entire Texas musical experience of the late 1970s and early 1980s. Lightnin' often lamented the death of all the original country bluesmen, but he also took delight in the young white audiences that revered his heritage and embraced his style.

One of the last of the great Texas bluesmen is in many ways the most intriguing. Mance Lipscomb, born in 1895 on a farm in the bottomland where the Navasota River converges with the Brazos, did not become recognized as a professional musician until his sixty-fifth year. From his father, a former slave, Mance learned to fiddle, and from his half-Choctaw mother he learned a sincere Christian faith and a cunning insight into human nature. Barely surviving as a sharecropper, Mance frequently played local dances or social gatherings in the Navasota area. But unlike the other rural bluesmen, he never made the move to Dallas or Houston. Mance stayed on the farm, got married before the First World War, and sat on his porch strumming an old pine guitar until he was discovered. That "discovery" was made in 1960 by Mack McCormick of KUHF radio station in Houston and Chris Strachwitz of Arhoolie Records, a San Francisco-based company devoted to preserving the old blues and jazz legends.

Mance was a songster in the tradition of Henry "Ragtime Texas" Thomas. It is much too restrictive to label him a blues singer; there was enormous diversity in his wide range of guitar skills and the wealth of material that filled his repertoire. He had a high baritone voice and a dexterity with the guitar strings that would be amazing for someone half his age. Mance was a folklorist in the finest sense of the word, and his blues ballads, breakdowns, reels, and shouts attest to a versatility that encompasses all facets of Texas culture. But there was more to Mance Lipscomb than his obvious musical brilliance; he had a simple and straightforward sincerity. Perhaps that quality overshadowed his music, for no one who ever met Mance or heard him perform walked away from the experience without having been moved by his warmth and gentleness. He was uneducated, but he was brilliant in his

Sam "Lightnin' " Hopkins at a recording session in the early 1960s. (*University of Texas Institute of Texan Cultures at San Antonio.*)

Kurt Van Sickle—in addition to being a close friend and admirer of Mance Lipscomb, Van Sickle today continues the Lipscomb tradition with his expert guitar stylings. *(Brian N. Kanof.)*

Texas songster Mance Lipscomb. *(Burton Wilson.)*

ability to understand others and touch them deeply.

Once Mance recorded his first cuts for Arhoolie Records, he literally became an overnight cult sensation. He appeared at folk festivals from Monterey to Newport, coffee houses from San Francisco to New York, and at folk-crazed university campuses nationwide. He played Austin more than any city in the country from the mid-1960s until 1974, at such diverse clubs as the Vulcan Gas Company, the Saxon Pub, and the Armadillo. Mance maintained that he taught two Austin musicians "to learn time" (rhythm), Janis Joplin and Mary Egan of Greezy Wheels. The tragedy of Mance's fourteen year musical career was that it was so brief. Mance's death in 1976 at the age of eighty, with his wife of sixty-three years and various musician friends at his side, was a loss to the world of music and to humanity.

The Texas bluesmen by no means invented the blues, nor did they lead the innovations that led the evolution of country blues to jazz. But their contribution is an enduring one, evidenced by the next generation that embraced their sound and style while simply adding an electric guitar. That next generation of musicians may have labeled themselves jazz artists or singers of rhythm and blues, but their music was also rooted in the Texas farmland. They are the legacy of the country bluesmen. Most of the original country bluesmen and blueswomen are now gone, but many of them did see their music take hold in America and grow to be enjoyed and respected. They saw their music become the backbone of that future phenomenon of American popular music, rock 'n' roll.

But the blues look backward to another time, another people. The image of a lonely figure surrounded onstage by only faint red and blue lights conjures up memories of the rural frustrations of Blind Lemon Jefferson, the urban alienation of Lightnin' Hopkins, the personal tragedy of Leadbelly, or the genuine kindness of Mance Lipscomb. The lives and music of these giants of Texas history echo the words spoken in 1964 at a music festival by America's greatest voice of human hope, Martin Luther King, Jr.:

> God has wrought many things out of oppression. He has endowed his creatures with the capacity to create, and from this capacity have flowed the sweet songs of sorrow and of joy that have allowed man to cope with his environment in many situations. . . .
>
> When life itself offers no order and meaning, the musician creates an order and meaning from the sounds of earth which flow through his instrument. . . .
>
> Much of the power of our Freedom Movement in the United States has come from this music. It has strengthened us with its powerful rhythms when courage began to fail. It has calmed us with its rich harmonies when spirits were down.

♬

Bob Wills—the King of western swing. (*Courtesy Dr. Charles Townsend.*)

5
Western-Swing

Deep within my heart lies a melody

Deep within my heart lies a melody
A song of old San Antone
Where in dreams I live with a memory
Beneath the stars all alone.

San Antonio Rose
Bob Wills

There appeared on the Texas plains and prairies in the late 1920s and early 1930s a new and innovative form of American popular music — an improvisational mix of country, jazz, blues, ragtime, folk, and a style to be known twenty-five years later as rock 'n' roll. It was the dance music of the Southwest, western-swing. Western-swing incorporated all of the ethnic influences prevalent in Texas: the country sound of the southern string bands, the rhythms of the blues- and jazz-oriented black culture, and a flavor of Mexican folk and mariachi music. It was a music characterized by experimentation and bound by no limits in style or direction. As an entertainment form, western-swing introduced the evolving rural Texas dance band tradition to the growing cities of the Southwest.

Dance music had always been important to the settlers who populated Texas throughout the nineteenth century. The southeastern custom of meeting at a neighbor's house, rolling back the carpet, and dancing Saturday night away was a common form of social activity on the Texas farm and ranch frontier. These "house parties" eventually gave way to larger and more organized barn dances. By the 1920s, however, the Texas style of dancing and the music that supported it had developed very distinct features that were in marked contrast with those of the Appalachian Mountains

or the cotton states of the Southeast. Texas dance music was a conglomerate of Anglo reels and square-dance steps, German polkas, Cajun swing, Mexican strolls and waltzes, and black jazz influences. The unique geographical, economic, and social environment in Texas created the ethnic interaction and defined this "new" music, which some labeled hillbilly jazz, Tex-Mex, country dance music, southwestern swing, or, as it came to be known nationwide, western-swing.

Texas possessed two resources that were not abundant in other parts of the South, cattle and oil. From the vast, sprawling cattle ranches came a Mexican influence in customs and mores that no doubt affected the musical tastes of the Texans. There was an isolation in ranch life that encouraged a more open, freewheeling atmosphere. This independent Texas lifestyle was coupled with a boom-or-bust mentality following the discovery of oil in East Texas near the turn of the century. The overnight growth of boom-town oil camps and refinery cities created a mobile, less-restrictive society. And many of the workers who now rode those Texas rigs were from Louisiana, and Louisiana meant jazz.

Another factor played a role in the social milieu that was Texas, and that was religion. The religious codes that dominated southeastern lifestyles were somewhat less repressive in Texas, and therefore conformity was viewed in some circles as more of a vice than a virtue. And although most Texans were a conformity-ridden people, that affliction was unheard of among the "fiddle bands" that played the barn dances and dance halls of Texas. It's as if the security of the older, mountainous region of the Southeast was less receptive to innovation; whereas the flat, wind-swept prairies invited or even demanded creativity.

The creativity of the Texas swing bands took form in an endless number of melodic variations. They were jazz-oriented and often emphasized the skill of one band member in what were usually called "take-off" solos. But the most visible difference between the western-swing tradition and the earlier country dance bands lay in instrumentation. The western-swing bands welcomed any and all instruments: a lead fiddle, tenor banjo, steel guitar, piano, drums, clarinets, saxophones, and sometimes an entire brass section. They were the Southwest's contribution to the Big Band era.

During the 1920s several Texas dance bands bridged the gap between the southeastern string-band tradition and western-swing. One of those groups was Prince Albert Hunt and the Texas Ramblers from Terrell. Hunt was regarded as one of Texas' finest breakdown fiddlers, and he was one of the first swing performers to record. His youth was spent in close contact with black musicians in and around his hometown just east of Dallas, and that no doubt accounted for his blues- and jazz-dominated fiddle style. Hunt and the Texas Ramblers were the biggest dance band draw in the Dallas area until Prince Albert was mysteriously shot to death following a 1931 performance.

Other dance bands moving toward the swing sound in the late 1920s included the Hi-Flyers, a group from Fort Worth led by Elmer Scarborough, and Oscar and Doc Harper's Band, two fiddlers who backed Prince Albert Hunt on his recordings with OKeh Records. In East Texas, near Lindale, another fiddle dance band was experimenting with jazz rags and popular music from other areas, the East Texas Serenaders. The leader of the Serenaders was a left-handed fiddler named Daniel Huggins Williams, a Tennessee native who brought the mountain sounds with him to Texas. Other members were tenor banjoist John Munnerlin, guitarist Claude Hammonds, and Henry Bogan, a bass player who improvised by using a three-string cello. The importance of the East Texas Serenaders was more than just symbolic, for their innovative instrumentals were recorded by Columbia, Brunswick, and Decca from 1927 to 1934. This was the period in which Texans began to expand their repertoires and utilize the enormous variety of sounds that surrounded them.

In identifying the birth and following the development of any social movement, there is usually a dominant figure who emerges as its symbol. In the case of Texas music's most distinctive style, western-swing, the symbol of the movement is the person who gave it its identity, defined its direction, and popularized it on a nationwide scale. That person was, of course, Bob Wills. The story of Bob Wills and of western-swing is the same.

James Robert Wills was born in 1905 on a farm in Limestone County near Kosse, Texas. Jim Rob, as he was known in his youth, grew up in a musical family — a family of "frontier fiddlers," as Wills' biographer, Dr. Charles Townsend, observed. But the major influence on the musical life of Bob Wills occurred when he was eight years old. His family

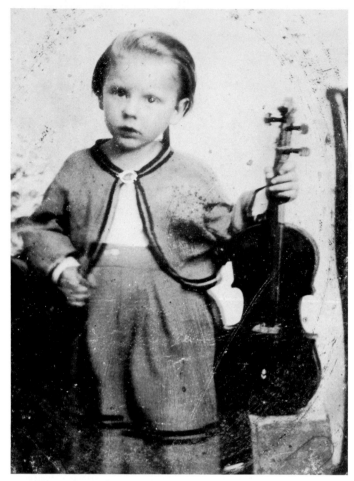

A fiddler on the Texas frontier. (*Photo from San Antonio Conservation Society. University of Texas Institute of Texan Cultures at San Antonio.*)

Laura Lee McBride — the "Queen of Western Swing." Her entire life has been devoted to the love and promotion of Texas music, from her own singing career, which began as Bob Wills' first female singer, to her relationship with two other prominent Texas musicians: her father, Tex Owens, and her husband, Dickie McBride. (*Courtesy of Leon and Chic Carter.*)

One of the first "swing" bands, the Hi-Flyers from Fort Worth. Their leader was Elmer Scarborough (second from left). *(Texas Music Collection.)*

moved to West Texas, and here Bob met the black musicians of the Texas plains with whom he served a musical apprenticeship. Wills embraced the country blues of the black Texans and then modified it in combination with the white fiddle music of the Southeast. The result was western-swing. It was the merging of two folk traditions that had existed side by side for three centuries in the American South.

Bob Wills left his hometown of Turkey, Texas, in 1929 and took up residence in Fort Worth. After a brief stint on radio station WBAP, Wills joined a traveling medicine show as a blackface minstrel. While working with Doc's Medicine Show in the Dallas–Fort Worth area, Bob met guitarist Herman Arnspiger and later paired up with him to form the Wills Fiddle Band. They played house parties and private dances in the North Texas region as well as performing on their own radio program six days a week. In the fall of 1930 Wills and Arnspiger teamed with two other musicians, Milton and Durwood Brown. The group then accepted an offer with WBAP, Fort Worth's most famous and powerful station. They changed their name to the Aladdin Laddies, and from that point their fame and reputation spread as fast as the enthusiasm for the new music they played, music dubbed by many as "western jazz."

Radio exposure meant more dances with larger crowds, and it led to the biggest break in Bob Wills' career. In 1931 Wills, Arnspiger, and Milton Brown went to work for station KFJZ in Fort Worth. Their morning program was sponsored by the Burrus Mill and Elevator Company and its major product, Light Crust Flour. It was not long before the band inherited the name, the Light Crust Doughboys. For the next year and a half the Doughboys ruled the radio airwaves, not only in Fort Worth but throughout the Southwest. Before the breakup of the original Doughboys, a number of prominent musicians joined their ranks, among them guitarist and tenor banjoist Sleepy Johnson, singer and yodeler Leon Huff, steel guitarist Leon McAuliffe, and Bob's brother Johnnie Lee Wills. There was another personality that was associated with the Light Crust Doughboys, W. Lee O'Daniel. O'Daniel was the general manager of Burrus Mill and became the band's master of ceremonies; he even wrote a number of songs performed and recorded by the Doughboys. "Pappy" O'Daniel rode the

coattails of the Light Crust Doughboys to statewide acclaim, and his radio popularity eventually gained him the governorship of Texas and a seat in the United States Senate.

Even though many people considered the Light Crust Doughboys a hillbilly band, their music encompassed a broad range of material, from patriotic songs to gospel, from traditional country to the popular songs of the day. But their emphasis was on instrumentals, and they featured a diverse program including Tex-Mex, Hawaiian songs, and New Orleans jazz. Unfortunately, much of their program time was consumed by the ramblings of O'Daniel in the form of poems, tributes, or sentimental propaganda that slowly built his political clout. Dissatisfaction with O'Daniel's obstinate and heavy-handed control of the Light Crust Doughboys led to the departure of the original members when they were at the peak of their success. The first to go was vocalist Milton Brown.

In 1932 Milton Brown created his own swing band, the Musical Brownies. The Brownies included Cecil Brower, Jesse Ashlock, Cliff Bruner, Ocie Stockard, Wanna Coffman, Papa Calhoun, Bob Dunn, and Durwood Brown. Various members of the band joined or left it at different times between 1932 and 1936, but they all were instrumental in moving the Texas dance band tradition toward the more experimental jazz sounds they had learned under Bob Wills tutelage. They were perhaps the most influential, if not the most popular, band in Texas by the time Milton Brown was killed in an automobile crash in 1936. The Musical Brown-

This is the earliest known photo of Bob Wills, fiddling here at the age of fourteen in 1919. To his right is his father, John Wills. *(Edna Wills Collection, courtesy Dr. Charles Townsend.)*

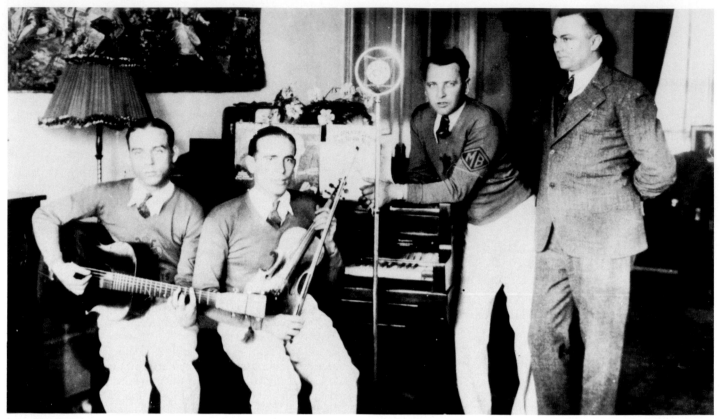

The Light Crust Doughboys in 1932 at the home of future governor W. Lee "Pappy" O'Daniel (left to right: Sleepy Johnson, Bob Wills, Milton Brown, W. Lee O'Daniel). *(Sleepy Johnson Collection, courtesy Dr. Charles Townsend.)*

Hank Thompson's forty-year career has embraced the two dominant sounds of Texas country music—honky-tonk and western-swing. *(Doug Hanners Collection.)*

ies did record on Decca Records and Bluebird Records before their demise, and the legacy of Milton Brown was carried on as the members of the Brownies joined or created other Texas dance bands in the 1930s and 1940s.

A year after Milton Brown left the Light Crust Dough-boys, Bob Wills followed his example. His new band, Bob Wills and his Playboys, consisted of Bob on fiddle, Johnnie Lee Wills on tenor banjo, Tommy Duncan on piano and vocals, Kermit Whalin on steel guitar and bass, June Whalen on rhythm guitar. The Playboys moved on to Waco, briefly tried Oklahoma City, and then traveled on to Tulsa. During their nine-year stay on radio station KVOO in Tulsa, Bob Wills and his Texas Playboys achieved their greatest artistic and commercial success. When their 1940 recording of *New San Antonio Rose* went gold, Wills and his band were firmly entrenched as the most famous western band in America, and consequently, the most famous dance band in American musical history.

The phenomenal public acceptance of Wills and the band was the result of a rare combination of music and personality. The music depended on a strong dance beat, dominated by Bob's heavily bowed fiddle and the jazz-oriented steel guitar style of Leon McAuliffe. Much of the Playboys' material was borrowed from the old fiddle songs of the rural South, songs such as *White River Stomp, Cotton Eyed Joe, Ida Red,* and *Stone Rag.* They also played the jazz favorites of the day like *St. Louis Blues, Basin Street Blues, I Ain't Got Nobody,* and *I Wish I Could Shimmy Like My Sister Kate.* Their catalog included western and Mexican hits such as *El Rancho Grande, South of the Border, My Adobe Hacienda, Oklahoma Hills,* and *Deep in the Heart of Texas.* And of course, the songs written by Bob Wills and his fellow

After leaving the Bob Wills band, steel guitarist Leon McAuliffe led his own successful western-swing band. He also wrote and made famous the country music classic *Steel Guitar Rag.* *(Doug Hanners Collection.)*

band members are American classics: *San Antonio Rose, Faded Love, Take Me Back to Tulsa, Eight'r From Decatur, Time Changes Everything,* and *Panhandle Rag.* Whatever the origin of the song, the Bob Wills arrangement had a jazz flavor. In simplest terms, that was what Bob Wills and the Texas Playboys were all about—a jazz dance band with country instruments.

But there was more to the success story of Bob Wills than the infectious dance music he produced. The secret of Wills' genius was an obvious one to those who saw him perform live; he was a master entertainer. As Wills punctuated the music with his familiar "Aaaha!" and "Take it away, Leon," the dance crowd was under his control. He provided a scarce commodity for southern and southwestern Americans during the thirties and forties, a good time.

Bob Wills and his band could not play every dance hall on a Texas Saturday night. Hundreds of swing bands appeared in the Southwest until the craze began to lose its appeal in the early 1950s. There were the Tune Wranglers, led by Buster Coward, and Adolph Hofner and his Texans from San Antonio. Roy Newman and His Boys, featuring Gene Sullivan on vocals, played out of Dallas. There were Doug Bine's Orchestra from Waco and Bob

Hank Thompson and his Brazos Valley Boys—voted the top western-swing band in the country for thirteen straight years during the fifties and sixties. *(Country Music Foundation.)*

Jimmy Heap and the Melody Masters. *(Mrs. Jimmy Heap.)*

Skyles' Skyrockets from Pecos. In Houston Ted Daffan and his Texans competed with The Village Boys, Shelley Lee Alley and His Alley Cats, Leon Selph and The Bar-X Cowboys. Cliff Bruner and the Texas Wanderers were headquartered in Beaumont, the Miller Brothers in Wichita Falls, and in Austin the major bands included Jack True's Nite Owls, Jesse James and his Boys, Doug Hullum and his Swing Boys. The Crystal Springs Ramblers were one of Fort Worth's major attractions. Hoyle Nix and the West Texas Cowboys waltzed across West Texas from their base in Big Spring. And the Blue Ridge Playboys, pioneers in the Texas honky-tonk sound, were known primarily as a swing band.

Alvin Crow. Alvin and the Pleasant Valley Boys are the premier western-swing dance band in Texas today. *(George and Carlyne Majewski.)*

Another group known for its versatility was Bill Boyd's Cowboy Ramblers from Greenville. Bill Boyd went on to earn a reputation as a singing cowboy, while two other members of the Ramblers later emerged as stars in their own right, Art Davis as a bandleader in Oklahoma and Jesse Ashlock as one of the finest improvisational fiddlers in Bob Wills' Texas Playboys.

Western swing reached its zenith in the late 1930s and through the war years. After World War II, there was a steady decline in its popularity except for a few of the larger, more established bands. Bob Wills was still extremely successful, but he was performing out of California at this time, not Texas. The demise of western-swing paralleled the demise of the Big Band era; there was a postwar rejection of the jazz-oriented dance bands all over the country. Country audiences were turning to the honky-tonk sounds of Texas and to new Nashville stars like Hank Williams. During the 1950s only a handful of western-swing bands survived. Johnnie Lee Wills, Bob's brother, had his own band that remained popular in the Oklahoma area. Tommy Hancock and the Roadside Playboys were prominent in the Lubbock area, performing at one time as the house band at the Cotton Club. Hoyle Nix and the West Texas Cowboys held on with continued success in West Texas. And one of the most durable of the fifties' dance bands was Jimmy Heap and the Melody Masters, based in Taylor, thirty miles northeast of Austin. Leon McAuliffe continued to do well on his own with his Cimarron Boys. But the unquestioned leader of western-swing in the 1950s — they were named top western-swing band for thirteen years — was Hank Thompson and the Brazos Valley Boys.

Henry "Hank" Thompson returned from World War II and formed a small honky-tonk band in his hometown of Waco. He slowly added more members to the band, the Brazos Valley Boys, and he also began to broaden the band's repertoire. The honky-tonk sound was polished and refined to reflect the pop music of the day. By the mid-fifties, the Brazos Valley Boys were the country's favorite western-swing band. In addition to profitable dance appearances, Hank Thompson had one of the biggest recording hits of the fifties, *The Wild Side of Life*.

Western-swing lay dormant for some twenty years despite the sporadic success of a few of its devotees. The Nashville sound, television, pop dance music, and rock 'n' roll all played a role in the decline of swing, but the apparent cyclical nature of American social trends and preferences took hold in the 1970s when a new generation of Texans discovered the music and legacy of Bob Wills — western-swing was born again.

The renaissance began in Austin and spread quickly across Texas. Throughout the seventies western-swing regained its national respectability, due in part to the simultaneous proliferation of Austin musicians combining all the diverse sounds of country and rock. Another factor that renewed interest in Bob Wills and his music was a critically acclaimed biography, *San Antonio Rose: The Life and Music of Bob Wills*, by Dr. Charles Townsend. Townsend examined Wills and western-swing from a scholar's perspective, and in so doing, he gave both Wills and American popular music credibility as subjects worthy of academic study. The honors for Bob Wills came rapidly with the revival of interest in western-swing. He was elected to the Country Music Hall of Fame, recorded one last album with many of the Playboys, and received numerous tributes before his death in

Asleep at the Wheel has achieved nationwide success in its promotion of western-swing. *(Scott Newton.)*

Two generations of western-swing excellence — Jesse Ashlock (formerly of Bob Wills and the Texas Playboys) and Alvin Crow in 1975. Also pictured are Bobby Earl Smith and Gary Roller (far right). *(Scott Newton.)*

Bob Wills and his Texas Playboys, 1937, (left to right: Everett Stover, trumpet; unidentified clarinet man; Zeb McNally, clarinet; Bob Wills, fiddle; Herman Arnspiger, guitar; Al Stricklin, piano; Smokey Dacus, drums; Tommy Duncan, vocals; Johnnie Lee Wills, banjo; Jesse Ashlock, fiddle; Sleepy Johnson, guitar; Joe Ferguson, bass; O.W. Mayo; Leon McAuliffe, steel guitar.) *(Courtesy Dr. Charles Townsend, from his book* San Antonio Rose: The Life and Music of Bob Wills.*)*

Milton Brown and his Musical Brownies rivaled Bob Wills for western-swing supremacy until Brown's accidental death in 1936.

(Courtesy Dr. Charles Townsend, from his book San Antonio Rose: The Life and Music of Bob Wills.*)*

Bob Wills and the Texas Playboys in Los Angeles, 1944. Laura Lee McBride was now singing with the Playboys. To her left is Bob Wills.

(Rip Ramsey Collection, courtesy Dr. Charles Townsend.)

1975. The last recording session for Bob Wills and the Texas Playboys occurred in December of 1973, and the resulting album, *For the Last Time*, led to a revival of the performing careers for the Playboys in the seventies and eighties. Among those continuing the Playboy tradition are Leon McAuliffe, Al Strickland, Smokey Dacus, Keith Coleman, Leon Rausch, Jesse Ashlock, and Johnny Gimble. Gimble, one of country music's busiest session men as well as Texas' most respected fiddler, has had the most visible success from his Nashville studio work to his legendary back up performances with Willie Nelson. The Playboys speak proudly when reliving their years with Bob Wills, but they are also quick to point to the new generation of swing artists who have perpetuated the western-swing heritage.

Among the hundreds of western-swing bands that appeared in the 1970s, two Austin-based groups have survived the Bob Wills imitators and the rapidly changing country scene: Asleep at the Wheel (led by Ray Benson), and Alvin Crow and the Pleasant Valley Boys. Asleep at the Wheel burst on the national scene in 1973 with their blend of western-swing, rock 'n' roll, and jazz. Their versatility was symbolic of the growing Austin sound of the early seventies; they were just as comfortable playing in a large jazz-oriented listening club in New York as they were in a West Texas honky-tonk. Ray Benson is the only original member of Asleep at the Wheel still with the group, and he has led them through a decade of hits like *Route 66, Miles and Miles of Texas, One o'Clock Jump*, and *The Letter That Johnny Walker Read*. Swing is the key ingredient in Asleep at the Wheel's performance, and no group does it better.

The other swing group that emerged from Austin in the early seventies, and one possessing the same durability and broad base of support as Asleep at the Wheel was Alvin Crow and the Pleasant Valley Boys. Alvin Crow left his native Oklahoma in 1968 and moved to Amarillo. For the next three years he played in several bands and began to experiment with combinations of country, rock, and western-swing. Then in 1971 Crow and his Amarillo band, the Pleasant Valley Boys, brought their country-rock act to Austin, where they became an integral part of the "progressive country" movement. Alvin Crow and the Pleasant Valley Boys have been one of the premier country dance bands in Texas through the seventies to the present. And although their forte is country swing and traditional Texas two-step, when Crow puts down his fiddle and picks up a guitar, the band can lay down a rockabilly set reminiscent of another group from the Texas Panhandle, Buddy Holly and the Crickets.

That versatility and willingness to employ the diversity of Texas music is the visible legacy of Bob Wills and western-swing. Swing was the cultural link between urban and rural, black and white, farm and factory; and it was a basis for the experimentation that characterized Austin music in the 1970s. The musical connection between the Texas of the 1930s and that of the seventies was best illustrated in the lyrics of a 1974 Waylon Jennings song:

**Well the honky-tonks in Texas were
    my natural second home.
Where you tip your hat to the ladies
    and the rose of San Antone.
I grew up on music that we call
    western swing,
It don't matter who's in Austin, Bob
    Wills is still the King.**

**Well if you ain't never been there
I guess you ain't been told,
That you just can't live in Texas
Unless you've got a lot of soul.**

**It's the home of Willie Nelson, the
    home of western swing,
He'll be the first to tell you, Bob
    Wills is still the King.**

Harry James—one of the most popular trumpeters and bandleaders of the Big Band era. *(Duncan Schiedt.)*

6

Jazz and The Big Bands

Then I'll know that something's happening

The thing I want to stay with is—jazz has got a beat. I want to look under the table and see a guy tapping his foot. And I want to look at the musician and see his vein popping out on his head. Then I'll know that something's happening.

Gene Ramey

Of all the varied forms prevalent in the world of popular music, jazz is the only one that is uniquely American in musical style and social symbolism—America's legitimate native contribution to the arts. It developed along the Mississippi River, grew spontaneously out of the syncopations of ragtime and the rhythms of the country blues, and then matured as it spread upriver from New Orleans to Memphis, St. Louis, Kansas City, and Chicago. As the proponents of jazz criss-crossed the Midwest and the Southwest with their "territorial bands" after World War I, Texas audiences and performers embraced the richness and excitement of the new sound—a sound that soon became the major musical expression of black culture in urban America.

The term *jazz* came into usage before World War I to denote melodic improvisation, discordant harmonies, and individualized tonal variations on the saxophone, clarinet, trombone, trumpet, or piano. The style itself has undergone a great number of changes, such as Dixieland, boogie-woogie, swing, bebop, Chicago-style, Kansas City-style, and free jazz. Throughout its sixty-five year history, however, jazz has retained elements from the sources that gave it birth: the rhythms indigenous to the southern slave experience, the harmonic and melodic qualities of southeastern folk music, and the style and emotion of the black church

spirituals, work songs, and minstrel shows. Since the geography and population of Texas contributed heavily to those sources, jazz correspondingly affected the social experiences of both black and white Texans, particularly in Dallas, San Antonio, and Houston. Even though only a few Texans were exposed to the spirit and energy of the music, the "jazz age" was very much a part of Texas in the 1920s.

Jazz dance bands proliferated in the cities of Texas and the Southwest from 1920 until 1940. The most successful of the early bands was the Alphonso Trent Orchestra. Trent's group was based in Dallas at the Adolphus Hotel, but it gained a national following while playing the dance circuit from the Mississippi Valley to New York City. The Alphonso Trent Orchestra was the nation's first black band to have a regular radio program, broadcasting over WFAA in Dallas. Membership in the Trent Orchestra included two of the early Texas jazz masters, Lawrence "Snub" Mosley (trombone) and Herbert "Peanuts" Holland (trumpet). Another trumpeter with Trent, Terrence Holder, left the group in 1925 and formed his own band, the Dark Clouds of Joy. Holder's band was also based in Dallas and rivaled his old boss for supremacy in the North Texas and Oklahoma region.

One of Texas' other dominant territorial bands of the

twenties was the Troy Floyd Orchestra. Floyd worked out of San Antonio's Shadowland Club, which was one of Texas' three major jazz ballrooms (along with the Rice Hotel in Houston and the Adolphus in Dallas). Often billed as Troy Floyd and his 10,000 Dollars Gold Orchestra, its personnel roster reads like a listing of Hall of Fame jazz greats. One of the soloists in Floyd's band was Claude "Benno" Kennedy, a trumpeter renowned by fellow musicians for his flashy and experimental style. In addition, Herschel Evans (tenor saxophone) and Buddy Tate (alto and tenor saxophone) later became stars with the Count Basie Orchestra and helped to found the Texas tenor sax tradition.

After the Troy Floyd Orchestra broke up, its trumpeter, Don Albert, reorganized the band and continued its residency at the Shadowland Club. Originally called Don Albert and his Ten Pals, the band became the premier jazz group of the 1930s and was eventually billed as Don Albert and his Music, America's Greatest Swing Band. Albert is one of the most important figures in the history of Texas jazz, not only because of his efforts as a pioneer in the San Antonio music scene, but also for his courageous, trailblazing policy of demanding integrated bands and audiences. He withstood the pressures of racism in the form of boycotts, raids, official harassment, and threats of violence. Albert's leadership encouraged hundreds of aspiring black, white, and brown musicians in the San Antonio area, but he also helped jazz gain acceptance as an entertainment form that could be enjoyed by any ethnic group.

As Albert achieved more fame and the one-night stands around the country became more frequent, another San Antonio ensemble filled the vacuum at home, Boots and his Buddies, led by "Boots" Douglas. Other cities around the state also seemed to have one band that served as the favorite of local dance fans. In Tyler, Eddie and Sugar Lou's Hotel Tyler Orchestra was the hottest group. Their trumpeter and vocalist, Oran "Hot Lips" Page, was a future legendary jazzman. Out in El Paso, the Blues Syncopaters monopolized the jazz dance scene. Their leader was Ben Smith (piano), and notable members included Debo Mills (drums) and Dan Minor (trombone). Amarillo was base for the Happy Black Aces, a major southwestern-territory band led by drummer Gene Coy. The featured performer for the Black Aces was Eddie Durham, a pioneer in the development of the electric guitar.

In Austin, the favorite jazz band was the DeLuxe Melody Boys. Austin was home for another important figure in the annals of American jazz, bass player Gene Ramey. His career began in the late twenties when he played tuba for George Corley and the Royal Aces in the Austin area. After switching to the bass, Ramey became one of the most respected jazzmen in Kansas City and New York over the next forty years. He has played with such greats as Charlie "Bird" Parker, Thelonius Monk, Stan Getz, and Miles Davis.

The most notable band in the Houston vicinity was the Milton Larkins Orchestra. Larkins played out of the Harlem Square Club and assembled a brilliant array of jazz performers: Arnett Cobb (tenor saxophone), Eddie "Cleanhead" Vinson (alto saxophone and vocals), and for a brief stint, Illinois Jacquet (tenor saxophone), and T-Bone Walker (guitar and vocals). Cobb, Vinson, and Jacquet became universally recognized as three of the finest saxophonists in the pre–World War II years, and all three had successful record-

The Phil Baxter Orchestra, pictured here in Dallas during the 1920s. *(Duncan Schiedt.)*

Don Albert. *(Duncan Schiedt.)*

ing careers with various groups and as soloists into the 1960s.

There were thriving jazz bands in every metropolitan region of Texas, but the heart of Texas jazz, and similarly, the birthplace of the Texas urban blues, was the Deep Ellum section of Dallas. While Alphonso Trent and Terrence Holder's orchestras were playing the downtown hotels or the suburban roadhouses (the Ozarks Club, Thomason Hall, and the Bagdad), the hidden and forbidden clubs and speakeasies along the northern part of Elm Street were the center of the blues and jazz action. The area was seething with music—jazz combos, jump bands, bebop and boogie-woogie pianists, blues and jazz vocalists, and street-corner guitarists. It was a magnet for musicians of every racial and cultural background, and therefore, symbolically and in vivid mu-

The Alphonso Trent Orchestra—house band at the Adolphus Hotel in Dallas through the twenties and thirties. *(Duncan Schiedt.)*

Troy Floyd Orchestra from San Antonio, 1928. *(Duncan Schiedt.)*

sical reality, Deep Ellum was the most visible example of the interaction of cultures that defines Texas music.

Many a jazz great served his or her apprenticeship in Deep Ellum. Some of the more notable combos playing there on a regular basis were the Voddie White Trio (featuring Buster Smith on clarinet), the Blue Moon Chasers, the Fred Cooper Band, and the Moonlight Melody Six. Deep Ellum was also home for many Texas women performers, particularly the great blueswomen who perfected their vocal craft with the jazz instrumentalists. Victoria Spivey, Sippie Wallace, and Big Mama Thornton each fronted a jazz group at one time or another in Deep Ellum. Monette Moore was even part of a trio, the Choo Choo Jazzers, that worked there exclusively before moving on to greater fame in New York.

The last survivor of the early Texas jazz bands to tour the country was the Ernie Fields Band. Fields was a trombonist from Nacogdoches who continued the territorial band tradition into the 1950s. Most of the remaining black dance bands broke up in the late thirties because of hard economic times, and then the outbreak of World War II virtually ended the era. The individual musicians migrated to New Orleans, Kansas City, or New York to pursue solo careers or to latch onto a new band.

The careers of the relatively few white jazz performers followed a similar scenario. But since there were a limited number of jazz proponents in the white community, those white musicians who dared to venture into the jazz world had widespread recognition and influence. The greatest white jazz performer from Texas was Weldon Leo (Jack) Teagarden. Born in Vernon, Jack Teagarden first picked up the trombone at the age of ten and joined his first jazz dance band at sixteen. Like the western-swing performers from the plains region, Teagarden's musical education came from a musically oriented family and the rhythmic sounds of his black neighbors. In his biography of Teagarden, *Jack Teagarden's Music*, Howard Waters relates one of Jack's early recollections:

> The spirituals I heard—the first ones I remember—were in Vernon, Texas, from a little colored revival under a tent in a vacant lot next door to our house. . . . These spirituals would build up until they'd fall on the ground. . . and they'd get their religion. . . . The singin' building up to this climax was really terrific. I'd sit out there on the picket fence we had and listen to it. And that seemed just as natural to me as anything. . . . I could hum along with 'em with no trouble at all.

Teagarden was part Indian and as a child had lived just across the Red River from the Indian territory of Oklahoma; his memories of that time were of a musical childhood:

> Once a year they used to have these Indian pow-wows. . . . When they would sing those Indian chants, you know, that came natural to me, too. I would embellish on that and I could play an Indian thing—just pick up my horn and play it to where you couldn't tell the difference. . . . I don't know how that came so natural.

A 1929 publicity photo of Ruby Roseína, a featured blues and jazz singer at the Shadowland Club in San Antonio. (San Antonio Light Collection. *University of Texas Institute of Texan Cultures at San Antonio.*)

Famed trumpeter Oran "Hot Lips" Page. *(Duncan Schiedt.)*

Don Albert's Ten Happy Pals, 1929. *(Duncan Schiedt.)*

Eddie Durham (left), from San Marcos, Texas, was the musician responsible for the development of the electric guitar. Also pictured are Lester Young and Walter Page. *(Duncan Schiedt.)*

Jack Teagarden's early career began with the Cotton Bailey Band at the Horn Palace Inn in San Antonio; he then moved to Shreveport, where he spent most of his free time listening to the black musicians in the roadhouses and brothels of Louisiana and East Texas. His love of black jazz and his lifelong friendships with black entertainers are well documented. In fact, he is often acknowledged as the first white jazz performer to record with black artists (5 March, 1929, *Knockin' a Jug*, with Louie Armstrong on trumpet and Jack Teagarden on trombone).

During the early 1920s, Teagarden joined the premier white bandleader in the Houston area, Peck Kelley. Kelley was a celebrity for years in Southeast Texas, and despite lucrative offers to record and perform elsewhere, he stayed in Texas and never made a record. But his career as leader of Peck's Bad Boys lasted beyond the World War II years, and his reputation as one of the most accomplished jazz pianists of his time was secure among his fellow musicians.

Teagarden played his trombone with Peck's Bad Boys for two years. Then, after a brief fling in the oil business, he joined the Southern Trumpeteers, a dance band performing at the Haven Tea Room in Wichita Falls. Throughout the twenties Jack changed bands regularly, but he spent several years off and on with another Texas band, Doc Ross and the Jazz Bandits. They had a number of successful stands in the Southwest (the Rice Hotel in Houston, Hotel Paso del Norte in El Paso, and Solomon's Penny Dance Arcade in Los Angeles). But ironically, since the jazz-oriented public prefered the black bands, the white performers had difficulty finding work and had to move on to the Northeast. White audiences were restricted to a very few local combos and the nationally renowned touring "big bands."

Jack Teagarden fell victim to the white prejudice against jazz in Texas and, like many of his black colleagues, he moved to New York. There he played with such classic big bands as the Dorsey Brothers Orchestra, the Paul Whiteman Orchestra, and the Louie Armstrong All-Stars. From 1939 on, Teagarden led his own jazz dance band. He continued to perform until his death in 1964 while he and his orchestra were performing in New Orleans. His career lasted over forty years, and his list of recordings is as lengthy as any in jazz history (over one thousand titles). Bebop trumpet great Red Rodney once recalled, "Jack's style seemed to take in all the known jazz schools. His mastery of the trombone was amazing. . . . Jack may well have been the greatest of all jazz trombonists."

Gene Ramey (bass) during his stint with the legendary Charlie "Bird" Parker. *(Gene Ramey Collection.)*

Buddy Tate, Dizzy Gillespie, and Gene Ramey — on the streets of Paris. *(Gene Ramey.)*

In addition to Peck Kelley and Jack Teagarden, there were other white Big Band leaders who had roots in Texas and acquired national followings. Phil Baxter and his Orchestra were a favorite in Dallas and the Midwest. The University of Texas had a nationally renowned dance band, Jimmie's Joys. And Gordon ("Tex") Beneke of Fort Worth gained fame as leader of the Glenn Miller Orchestra after a stint as Miller's tenor sax man. But the Texan who achieved the greatest recognition during the Big Band era was Harry James. The famed trumpeter grew up in Beaumont and began his career with a local group called the Old Phillips Friars. After joining national touring orchestras led by Ben

Pollack and Benny Goodman, James organized his own band in 1939. His success reached a peak in the 1940s, but he continued touring and recording into the 1970s. James' live performances were always heavily steeped in original jazz material, but his greatest public acclaim came from his pop-oriented recordings of the fifties, such as *You Made Me Love You, It's Been a Long, Long Time,* and *Three Coins in the Fountain.*

Two other Texas musicians had a dramatic impact on the jazz world, pianist Teddy Wilson and guitarist Charlie Christian. Both were introduced to mainstream Big Band audiences by Benny Goodman. Goodman was the first well-known bandleader to break the color barrier in the segregated clubs and dancehalls that existed in every section of the country in the 1930s. Often described as the "greatest pianist of the swing era," Teddy Wilson played with such jazz luminaries as Goodman, Lionel Hampton, Gene Krupa, Louie Armstrong, and Billie Holiday. Wilson was born in Austin in 1912 to a musical family; his brother Gus was a trombonist and arranger and played for years in the Central Texas area. In 1939, he formed the Teddy Wilson Orchestra, and although it was never as popularly received by the public as other bands of the period, it was regarded by Wilson's contemporaries as one of the most musically proficient bands of the jazz age. In the words of Benny Goodman, "Whatever elegance means, Teddy Wilson is it."

Benny Goodman brought another jazz legend to the public's attention in 1939 when he employed Dallas-born Charlie Christian. Christian died in 1942, but in that short span he earned a reputation as the most innovative of all jazz guitarists. Christian was first of the modern jazzmen to utilize single-string solos on the electric guitar — the integral link between the swing era of jazz and the coming bebop style of rhythm and blues. And though Texan Eddie Durham was the first jazzman to explore the electrical amplification of the guitar, Charlie Christian perfected it and served as the stylistic master for the coming generation of rhythm and blues and rock 'n' roll.

The Big Band dance craze died a slow death after World War II, but the Texas tenor sax school was well entrenched as a jazz tradition. That school of Texas innovators included Arnett Cobb, Herschel Evans, Buddy Tate, Eddie "Cleanhead" Vinson, Illinois Jacquet, Budd Johnson, Buster Smith, Charles Pillars, and Hayes Pillars, several of whom are still performing today. In the fifties and sixties a second generation of tenor saxophone men appeared to continue the tradition and expand the style: King Curtis (Curtis Ousley from Fort Worth), James Clay (Dallas), Gerald Stewart ("the best tenor player in East Texas"), John Handy (Dallas), Booker Ervin (Denison), David "Fathead" Newman (Dallas), and two Fort Worth products, Ornette Coleman and Dewey Redman.

Ornette Coleman was born in 1930 and was basically a self-taught musician. In the 1960s, he became the leading exponent of free jazz. Coleman's trademark is a complete freedom to improvise and experiment within the framework of every performance, and his adventurous directions have received their share of criticism from some traditionalists. But the Coleman method of atonality and random composition reaches back to the free spirit and improvisational stylings that created the blues, ragtime, and eventually led to jazz itself. Coleman expressed his approach to music on the liner notes of his album, *Ornette Coleman: Change of the Century:*

Houston's favorite dance band of the 1930s, the Milton Larkins Orchestra. *(Duncan Schiedt.)*

Arnett Cobb playing with Lionel Hampton's Band. *(Duncan Schiedt.)*

Jack Teagarden, 1920. *(Duncan Schiedt.)*

Ornette Coleman—the innovative leader of the free jazz movement. *(Courtesy of Antilles Records, photo by Steven Needham.)*

Dewey Redman. *(Courtesy of ECM Records.)*

Teddy Wilson accompanies Benny Goodman. *(Duncan Schiedt.)*

I don't tell the members of my band what to do. I let everyone express himself just as he wants to. The musicians have complete freedom, and so, of course, our final results depend entirely on the musicianship, emotional make-up and taste of the individual member.

Another of today's leaders of the Texas tenor sax contingent and a boyhood friend of Ornette Coleman in Fort Worth is Dewey Redman. Perhaps not as experimental as Coleman, Redman remains one of the most respected performers within the jazz world, often labeled "the musician's musician." His latest recordings indicate that he is ready to emerge from the shadow of Coleman and achieve the stardom his fellow musicians have long claimed he deserves.

One of the most commercial jazz groups to come from Texas in the last two decades is the Crusaders. They originally emerged from Houston's Fifth Ward with a variety of names—the Nite Hawks, Chitterling Circuit, and the Swingsters. While attending Texas Southern University, they changed their name to the Jazz Crusaders. As the Crusaders, they scored their biggest hit in 1966, *Uptight.* Their sound is slicker today—reflecting the polish of sound studios and California sidemen—but the urban emotion that sprang from the clubs on Dowling Street in downtown Houston is still there.

Peck Kelly (lower left) and the Bad Boys, mid-1930s. *(Duncan Schiedt.)*

Charlie Christian at work with the electric guitar while performing with the Benny Goodman Band. *(Duncan Schiedt.)*

Joe Sample (left) and Wilton Felder of the Crusaders. *(Courtesy of MCA Records.)*

Tomás Ramírez, 1980. (Photo by Scott Newton, courtesy of "Austin City Limits.")

Passenger in performance on "Austin City Limits," 1981. *(Photo by Scott Newton, courtesy of Austin City Limits.)*

Don Albert (left) and Herschel Evans. *(Duncan Schiedt.)*

The ethnic experiences of the Mexican-American community also found expression in jazz and Big Band dance styles. Especially in the late forties and early fifties, Cuban and Mexican rhythms began to infiltrate many of the jazz dance bands around the country. The Texans had a unique jazz style to complement this national trend in recordings and the movies. The Tex-Mex bands (the *conjunto* bands) retained their regional flavor, but imagery and labels aside, much of what they played was pure jazz. Some of the leading groups of that period were Beto Villa (featuring Wally Armendáriz, Luis Gasca, and Roy Montelongo), Isidro López, and Los Alegres de Terán. Texas jazz artists like Luis Gasca and Joe Gallardo continued this tradition into the sixties and seventies and took the Tex-Mex jazz sound to international audiences.

Jazz has never held a prominent position in the musical tastes of the Texas masses. But it has witnessed a steady growth since the late 1960s, resulting in part from the maturing of the rock generation which sought an expansion of musical directions and influences. The fusion of jazz and rock has created a new musical discipline—one in which several Texans play dominant roles. Three of the rising stars in the jazz-rock field include Texas-born Larry Coryell, Ronnie Laws, and Will Lee.

In the last ten years, the jazz scene within the borders of Texas has exploded. Jazz orchestras can be found on every college campus; jazz societies promote the art in Dallas and Houston; and the healthiest example of live jazz anywhere in the Southwest is located in Austin. The Austin-based jazz bands often defy description—producing a blend of jazz, rock, rhythm and blues, and reggae. The Austin roster of jazz groups includes Beto y los Fairlanes (led by Robert Skiles), Extreme Heat, the Jazzmanian Devils, Minor Miracle (with Carmen Bradford), Dan del Santo and his Professors of Pleasure, the Rich Harney Trio, and the premier jazz group in Texas, Passenger. The most respected performer in the Austin jazz community is saxophonist Tomás Ramírez. Steeped in the *conjunto* tradition of his native South Texas, the talent of Ramírez rivals and perhaps exceeds that of the long line of historical Texas saxophonists, ranking him as one of America's finest musical performers.

Jazz, as its nature suggests, is constantly changing and responding to the artistic needs of the musician. It is basically a musician's medium—one that has had a stormy history in Texas, but one that has survived. The rebirth of jazz in Texas in the seventies and eighties has by no means challenged rock or country, but it has proved that there is a place in Texas for musical innovation and artistic freedom of expression—that is the essence of jazz.

♫

Charlie Christian — the pioneer in the development of the electric guitar, 1940. *(Texas Music Collection.)*

7

Rhythm and Blues

They call it stormy Monday, but Tuesday's just as bad

They call it stormy Monday, but
Tuesday's just as bad,
They call it stormy Monday, but
Tuesday's just as bad,
Wednesday's worse, Lord Thursday's
oh so sad.

They Call It Stormy Monday
Aaron ''T-Bone'' Walker

Rhythm and blues was originally the music of the ghetto—a vibrant black art form that sprang from the streets of America's segregated cities. Universally acknowledged as the father of rock 'n' roll, rhythm and blues is now revered by anyone who seeks an emotional fervor and a gut-wrenching earthiness in his or her music. It is a music whose sound and style embody a hope of liberation from the pressures and frustrations of the modern urban experience. The Texas rhythm and blues tradition, which grew primarily out of Dallas and Houston, provided the major transitional figures who began the American R and B revolution after World War II and helped bring it to fruition in the 1960s.

Until the late 1940s, any performance by a black entertainer—whether it be pop, jazz, bebop, swing, or Big Band—was labeled "race music." Rhythm and blues appeared as a euphemism for "race" after the war when black veterans poured into the nation's large cities and subsequently became an economic and social force. Social conditions in Texas created an especially fertile ground for the development of the urban blues. Texas possessed several of the South's most populous cities, viewed as havens of opportunity by black men and women just one generation removed from the country-blues tradition. Most of these

aficionados of the rural blues style were isolated in the racial "wards" of Dallas, Houston, Fort Worth, and San Antonio. This ghetto atmosphere, coupled with the repressive Texas penal system and brutal sharecropping economy, was the incentive for the intensity, vitality, and spirit of rhythm and blues, Texas style.

Like its first cousins, jazz and the country blues, R and B was spawned from the Afro-American slave experience and the climate of oppression that black Americans have faced both on the farm and in the factory. One training ground for the R and B artists that emanated from this tradition was the church—Protestant singing factories that produced superstars every Sunday morning. Their gospel shouts and wails provided an emotional continuity as R and B developed throughout the 1930s and 1940s. The gospel link remained strong as the jazz performers took over the large dance arenas and concert halls and the R and B men and women moved into the smaller clubs and cabarets. It was a strange alliance—modified black spirituals ringing through smoke-filled ghetto taverns. But the music and its message provided the same sense of fulfillment and self-esteem for the black community as the sermons and scriptures intermittently spaced between the powerful gospel songs during Sunday services.

The most notable development in the evolution of rhythm and blues from its rural and religious roots was the amplification of the acoustic guitar. The two leading figures in the utilization of this new technology, the electric guitar, were Eddie Durham (from San Marcos) and Charlie Christian (from Dallas). Durham's use of a resonator on his guitar in 1935 produced the first recording using an amplified guitar. Two years later he met Charlie Christian, and Christian brought the instrument and its unique sound to the world of jazz while playing with the Benny Goodman Orchestra. Both Durham and Christian were the pioneers of the electric guitar, but the performer who combined its use with the blues combo—and in doing so created the basic framework for rhythm and blues and the resulting format of the rock 'n' roll bands—was Aaron "T-Bone" Walker.

T-Bone Walker was the most important and influential musician in the history of rhythm and blues, and perhaps in the history of all its derivative styles, including rock 'n' roll. Walker was born in Linden, Texas, in 1910, but he was raised in the Oak Cliff section of Dallas. A product of the city, T-Bone witnessed the country blues-

Albert Collins learned his blues in rural Texas and perfected them in downtown Houston. *(Steve Salibo, courtesy of Angela Strehli.)*

men singing for pennies on the corners of South Dallas, the ragtime orchestras that headlined the medicine shows and carnivals, and the gospel shouters who sang for salvation in the tent revivals. T-Bone's musical baptism began early in a small, white frame Baptist church hidden behind an old housing project in Oak Cliff. He described that experience in Arnold Shaw's *Honkers and Shouters:*

> The first time I ever heard a boogie-woogie piano was the first time I went to church. That was the Holy Ghost Church in Dallas. . . . We all learned our blues in the church. That's where the music was.

Walker first recorded for Columbia under the pseudonym "Oak Cliff T-Bone." Those early recordings (*Wichita Falls Blues* and *Trinity River Blues*) bore a striking similarity to the work of Blind Lemon Jefferson—no coincidence, as Jefferson was a friend of the family and had played numerous times with T-Bone and his stepfather. For the next six years Walker had a variety of musical experiences, including stints with the Haines Circus, the Count Biloski Band (a white jazz dance band), Coley Jones' Dallas String Band, and several other vaudeville acts in the Dallas area. Sometime around 1935 T-Bone met Charlie Christian and began experimenting with the electric guitar. Later that year T-Bone moved to Los Angeles, and it was there that he first used the electric guitar in combination with the traditional blues combo (usually consisting of tenor saxophone, string bass, and piano). It was an innovation that began the modern era of rhythm and blues.

T-Bone Walker's legendary status among American musi-

Aaron "T-Bone" Walker—his innovations on the electric guitar and his development of the blues combo began the modern era of rhythm and blues. *(Amy O'Neal, courtesy of* Living Blues *magazine.)*

cians emanates from his advanced guitar techniques (harmonic chording and jazz-influenced arpeggio runs) and his distinctive flair for showmanship. His forty-year career left an indelible mark on every musician who ever picked an electric guitar. Today's leading figure in rhythm and blues, B. B. King, reflected in *Honkers and Shouters* on the impact that Walker has had on his career:

> When I first heard T-Bone's single string solo on *Stormy Monday*, it drove me crazy. I could never believe a sound could be that pretty on an instrument. . . . T-Bone has a way of using ninth chords— nobody's done it ever yet. . . . I like his singing, too, but he always killed me with the guitar. Just completely killed me.

During the early 1940s T-Bone Walker played with several jazz-oriented dance orchestras (the most prominent being the Les Hite Orchestra), but in 1945 he ventured out as a soloist and eventually assembled his own R and B band. Walker's success peaked in the post-war years in Los Angeles; it was there that new independent record labels originated and were willing to record the R and B fusion of jazz, boogie-woogie, and the country blues. A number of other Texans were at the forefront of the resulting rhythm and blues explosion—a Texas-California connection that transformed rhythm and blues from an isolated urban sound in the forties to the dominant music of the black community. There were pianists Charles Brown, Floyd Dixon, Amos Milburn, Monette Moore, Lloyd Glenn, Robert Smith, and Ivory Joe Hunter. The list of prominent R and B guitarists includes Li'l Son Jackson, Smokey Hogg, PeeWee Crayton, Frankie Lee Sims, Peppermint Harris, Walter Brown, Curtis Jones, Juke Boy Bonner, Bee Houston, Johnny "Guitar" Watson, Lawyer Houston, R. S. Rankin (Little T-Bone), Lowell Fulson, Albert Collins, and Freddie King. And many of the Texas tenor sax greats were equally at ease with R and B combos as with jazz bands, especially King Curtis and Eddie "Cleanhead" Vinson.

While the male bluesmen were extracting the sound of the urban soul from their instruments, Texas women were establishing a notable rhythm and blues tradition with their vocal performances and recordings. The major country blues stars, Victoria Spivey and Big Mama Thornton, achieved their greatest fame fronting rhythm and blues bands, Spivey in New York and Thornton in Chicago. Sippie Wallace, Hociel Thomas, Maggie Jones, and Monette Moore continued to perform their blend of country-gospel-blues to the accompaniment of electrically charged rhythm and blues bands. But during the R and B boom of the fifties and early sixties a new generation of Texas blueswomen appeared; the two dominant Texas R and B singers of that era were Esther Phillips and Barbara Lynn.

Esther Phillips (born in Galveston) began her singing career in Los Angeles with Johnny Otis' Rhythm and Blues Caravan. Billed as "Little Esther," she had toured the nation's clubs and auditoriums before she reached the age of twenty. After a self-imposed early retirement, Esther made a comeback in the sixties and has remained one of the premier R and B performers. In 1974 and 1975 she received awards from *Ebony* and *Rolling Stone* magazines as the best female rhythm and blues singer in the industry.

Bee Houston at a recording session, 1958. *(Chris Strachwitz, Arhoolie Records.)*

Barbara Lynn, often regarded as the "Queen of Texas Rhythm and Blues" in the sixties, is somewhat more pop-oriented than Esther Phillips. Based in her hometown of Beaumont, Barbara Lynn had substantial crossover success in the 1960s with blues-rock recordings. Under the guidance of producer Huey Meaux, Lynn had a giant hit with *You'll Lose a Good Thing* in 1961 and followed it up with *You're Gonna Need Me* and *Oh Baby*. The Motown stars of the early sixties overshadowed Barbara Lynn on a national scale, but her years of continued success on the R and B charts indicate her enormous talent and versatility as a song stylist and blues guitarist.

Any survey of Texas rhythm and blues must include the contribution of Don D. Robey, Texas' most prolific and suc-

Clarence "Gatemouth" Brown and Aaron "T-Bone" Walker. *(Texas Music Collection.)*

Big Mama Thornton and the Chicago Blues Band. To Big Mama's left is one of America's blues legends, Muddy Waters. *(Jim Marshall, Arhoolie Records.)*

Juke Boy Bonner has written some of Texas' finest urban blues, classics like *It's a Struggle Here in Houston. (Chris Strachwitz, Arhoolie Records.)*

cessful R and B entrepreneur. For over twenty years his Houston-based recording and publishing companies rivaled the Memphis, New York, and Los Angeles firms for R and B supremacy. Robey owned the Bronze Peacock Club in Houston and from there kept tabs on public tastes as well as the local talent. To capitalize on the wealth of talent showcased by his club, he first formed Peacock Records to record black gospel music. Robey and the Peacock label struck gospel gold with two Houston groups, the Mighty Clouds of Joy and the Dixie Hummingbirds. Robey also hit the top of the gospel charts with the Five Blind Boys and the Bells of Joy. In 1953, Robey expanded his recording empire with the creation of Duke Records, a rhythm and blues label that existed until 1973.

The prosperity of Don Robey's Duke Records resulted from the success of two Memphis artists, Bobby "Blue" Bland and Junior Parker. But while Bland and Parker brought national recognition to Robey and his organization, there were other performers who had sporadic hits on the label which insured Houston's claim as the center of Texas rhythm and blues. Big Mama Thornton recorded her hit, *Hound Dog*, in 1953 on Duke. Two transplanted Arkansas bluesmen, Larry Davis and Fenton Robinson, also achieved their greatest success with Duke. Davis wrote one of the classic Texas R and B cuts, *Texas Flood*. Other Duke performers were O. V. Wright, Buddy Ace, Marie Adams, Clarence "Gatemouth" Brown, and Johnny Ace. Johnny Ace (John Alexander) was a rising young star who died while playing Russian roulette backstage before a show on Christmas Eve in 1954 at the Houston City Auditorium. Little Richard also recorded on Duke just before he hit national stardom with *Tutti-Frutti* in 1955.

Ivory Joe Hunter—a legendary blues pianist. *(Huey Meaux Collection.)*

Rhythm and blues barely survived as a commercial enterprise during the late fifties and early sixties. It was a testament to Don Robey's business skill and musical intuition that Duke Records could compete with the white rock 'n' roll artists dominating the Texas market. Robey even had to contend with black prejudice against the R and B style. He once commented on this bias held by many black Texans: "In those days, rhythm and blues was felt to be degrading, low, and not to be heard by respectable people." But when the soul sound of the mid-sixties began to hit the national charts, and when white rockers began to discover their musical roots, rhythm and blues underwent a commercial revival comparable to its burgeoning growth after World War II. Don Robey's productions, as well as a number of Texas R and B legends, were in part responsible for the renewed interest in rhythm and blues that continued through the seventies and today is stronger than ever.

The Texas bluesmen who led the revitalized R and B scene were all disciples of T-Bone Walker — the three most prominent being Freddie King, Albert Collins, and Lowell Fulson. Lowell Fulson was born and raised in Oklahoma to a guitar-playing mother and a Cherokee father, but his musical career brought him to the Fort Worth and Dallas area in the early forties. During his teenage years, Fulson patterned his blues style after Blind Lemon Jefferson and Texas Alexander as he traveled and performed across Oklahoma and the Texas Panhandle. Later he discovered the electric guitar techniques of T-Bone Walker and PeeWee Crayton (from Austin) and the boogie piano style of Ivory Joe Hunter (from Port Arthur). The Lowell Fulson list of hits over the last thirty years makes him one of the most distinctive and innovative guitar stylists in R and B: *Blue Shadows, Lonesome Christmas, Reconsider Baby,* and *Every Day I Have the Blues.*

Albert Collins is another of the Texas rhythm and blues greats who helped continue the T-Bone Walker tradition into the sixties and seventies. Even though Collins spent his early years on a cotton farm in East Central Texas (Leon County), he was a product of the flowering R and B atmosphere that originated in Houston in the late forties. Albert started his own rhythm and blues combo (the Rhythm Rockers) while still a teenager in inner-city Houston. He established his musical reputation working with such notable Gulf Coast R and B and jazz performers as Malcolm Moore, Piney Brown, and Gatemouth Brown. Collins is now in his fourth decade as an entertainer and still transporting the classic Houston R and B sound around the world — from Antone's in Austin to the Montreux Jazz Festival in Switzerland.

The blues guitarist most responsible for the renewed ap-

"Little Esther"—Esther Phillips—has had three decades of commercial success on the R and B charts as well as several cross-over hits in the rock field. *(Amy O'Neal, courtesy* Living Blues *magazine.)*

Duke Records offered the Three Lamp Sisters as competition to the Motown female stars of the mid-sixties. *(Doug Hanners Collection.)*

Clarence "Gatemouth" Brown. *(Norbert Hess, courtesy of* Living Blues *magazine.)*

Barbara Lynn, appearing on Dick Clark's "American Bandstand" in 1963. *(Huey Meaux Collection.)*

preciation of rhythm and blues in Texas—from his powerful 1969 appearance at the Texas International Pop Festival to his legendary performances at the Armadillo World Headquarters in Austin—was Freddie King. King (Billy Myles) was born in 1934 in Gilmer amidst the fertile country blues territory of Northeast Texas. His mother (Ella Mae King) and his uncle (Leon King) were both active participants in that rural Texas heritage—both were guitarists who often performed at family gatherings or church picnics and passed their skills on to their children. At the age of sixteen Freddie King moved to Chicago and for the next eight years was part of the dynamic Chicago R and B club scene during the 1950s. After his first major hit in 1961, *Hideaway*, King returned to Texas and settled in Dallas. For the next fifteen years, until his death in 1976, Freddie King was the most prominent symbol of the Texas urban blues sound. And without question, he was the artist who brought that R and B sound to the young, white audiences who continued the Texas blues tradition into the seventies and eighties.

Freddie King was joined in the rebirth of R and B by hundreds of Texas urban blues performers. In the Houston and Gulf Coast region, the premier bluesman is Johnny Copeland. Another Houston product is blues guitarist Joey Long (at one time having served as instructor to such guitarists as Billy Gibbons of ZZ Top, and Johnny Winter). In the Fort Worth area, Robert Ealey has been a dominant artist for the last twenty years. The major bluesman in El Paso is a master vocalist and guitarist, Long John. Austin has provided two quality women blues pianists whose jazz credentials extend back three decades, Ernie Mae Miller and Ge-

Lowell Fulson in performance at the Armadillo World Headquarters in Austin, 1972. *(Burton Wilson.)*

Blues Boy Hubbard—a long-time proponent of Austin rhythm and blues. *(Steve Goodson, courtesy of Diana and Paul Ray.)*

neva Rawlings. Blues Boy Hubbard is another landmark of the Austin blues scene. And two Texas-Louisiana entertainers have had a tremendous impact on a national scale, Clarence "Gatemouth" Brown and Clifton Chenier. From his Cajun base in Louisiana and Southeast Texas, Chenier, the "King of Zydeco," has worked the R and B, jazz, and rock circuits since the 1940s. Gatemouth Brown, although born in Louisiana, grew up near Orange and has ventured into every facet of Texas music. He worked as a country singer in Nashville, played bass in a jazz dance band, formed his own Cajun dance combo, and starred for years as the featured R and B guitarist at Don Robey's Bronze Peacock Club in Houston. Gatemouth's performances run the spectrum from Cajun festivals to Willie Nelson picnics to rhythm and blues taverns on the Gulf Coast.

Rhythm and blues achieved a new respectability in the late sixties with the culmination of the civil rights movement and the emergence of black pride and power. The social implications inherent in the black revolution (an end to segregation, black political success, economic advances for blacks) paralleled the proliferation of black art and culture in the white community. The most visible example of this "cultural crossover" was soul music. Soul music was a pop-oriented derivative of rhythm and blues that was closely allied with the strongly rhythmic, mellow rock sound. Most of the soul productions were based in Detroit and New York, but Texas provided its usual share of quality artists. Sly Stone from Dallas had the greatest national success in the late sixties with his soul-rock performances. Joe Tex of Baytown was Texas' most consistent soul hit maker—for ten years he kept atop the soul charts with records like *Show Me* and *Hold What You've Got*. From Houston came Archie Bell and the Drells, a soul group whose lively dance beat hit *Tighten Up* foreshadowed the future disco sound. One of the most successful Texas soul singers was Barry White from Galveston. White and his Love Unlimited Orchestra, with his sultry vocal delivery and highly orchestrated ballads, survived fifteen years of change in the volatile soul and R and B market.

Soul music and the subsequent disco craze of the mid-seventies were related to, but actually existed outside of, the traditional limits of rhythm and blues. However, all of the forms that grew out of black American culture helped disintegrate the labeling and the restrictions that have continually plagued "black" music. As more and more white musicians began performing the blues, this stereotyping and categorization broke down to an even greater degree. As always, the musicians rejected attempts by the marketing arm of the industry or the public to pigeonhole their work. With the growth and spread of rhythm and blues in Texas during the seventies and eighties, it became especially difficult to define musical styles—to define the line that separated rock from rhythm and blues. Perhaps the process began when hard rockers like Janis Joplin and Johnny Winter proclaimed and exhibited their allegiance to the blues. And no doubt the phenomenon continues into the eighties as the Austin musical environment is dominated by quality R and B talent that experiments with innovative combinations of rhythm and blues, rock, jazz, and country. But that musical conglomerate is nothing new to Texas audiences; the master of that hybrid sound, Delbert McClinton, has been on the scene for twenty-five years.

Like a seemingly endless number of modern Texas musi-

Freddie King helped rekindle interest in rhythm and blues in the 1970s with appearances at traditional rock concert halls. Here he is performing at the Armadillo World Headquarters—often referred to as "the house that Freddie built." *(Burton Wilson.)*

cians, Delbert McClinton was born in Lubbock. But Delbert grew up in Fort Worth, and that was where he learned the blues. It was there he formed his first R and B band at the age of seventeen, the Straightjackets. The Straightjackets played the strip along the Jacksboro Highway—a mesh of country honky-tonks and black R and B clubs that sent the Fort Worth crime rate spiraling every Saturday night. Delbert and his band were regulars at Jack's Place on Fort Worth's northwest side, but they often landed gigs backing many of the great blues guitarists who played the R and B circuit from Chicago to Kansas City into Texas. After the Straightjackets disbanded, Delbert spent a brief period recording and touring with Bruce Channel (he played harmonica on Channel's hit *Hey Baby*). It was on that tour that Delbert reportedly taught John Lennon to play the harmonica. In the early sixties he found success on the rock charts as a member of the Rondells. A decade passed before his solo career took off with such albums as *Victim of Life's*

Circumstances, Second Wind, Keeper of the Flame, and *Plain' From the Heart.*

Delbert's act has always possessed a special intimacy—a brand of rock, country, and rhythm and blues accentuated by an infectious passion for the music and the audience. That intense emotion can best be witnessed in the small dance clubs where Delbert has perfected his craft over the last two decades, clubs like Soap Creek Saloon in Austin, Delbert's symbolic musical home and his favorite place to perform in Texas. But as his success mushrooms in the eighties and the crowds get larger, the honky-tonk performances become more infrequent. It is a familiar routine in Austin where, in the last ten years, many of the nation's most promising musicians have used the local music scene as a training ground. And it's likely the current crop of Texas blues artists will follow the same pattern as they gain national star status.

The Austin assembly of blues artists is a multitalented ag-

"Bongo Joe" George Coleman is a familiar fixture on the streets of Galveston, Houston, and San Antonio. Bongo Joe has played his oil drum rhythms in Texas for over two decades. *(Chris Strachwitz, Arhoolie Records.)*

Lou Ann Barton. *(Dennie Tarner.)*

The rhythm and blues rock 'n' roll of Storm from a 1972 concert at the Hungry Horse, Austin (left to right: Paul Ray, Doyle Bramhall, Jeff Barnes, Ed Vizard, Jimmie Vaughan, and Lewis Cowdrey). *(Burton Wilson.)*

Clifton Chenier—the "King of Zydeco". *(Michael Smith, courtesy Arhoolie Records.)*

An early seventies Austin blues band, Hard Times (left to right: W. C. Clark, Angela Strehli, Denny Freeman, Andy Miller, and Alex Napier). *(Burton Wilson.)*

The Cobras (left to right: Alex Napier, Paul Ray, Denny Freeman, Stevie Ray Vaughan, Joe Sublett, and Rodney Craig). *(Photo by* *Debbe Sharpe, courtesy of Diana and Paul Ray.)*

Jimmie Vaughan of the Fabulous Thunderbirds. *(Dennie Tarner.)*

Kim Wilson of the Fabulous Thunderbirds. *(Dennie Tarner.)*

Katie Webster—Queen of the Swamp Blues Piano. Pictured at left is Denny Freeman, and right, Keith Ferguson. *(Susan Antone)*

gregation of musicians who discovered their R and B roots in the glory days of Texas rock 'n' roll. While many of their colleagues were moving toward country-rock in the early seventies, they embraced the other end of the Texas musical spectrum, rhythm and blues. Foremost among the Austin bands, and arguably the premier blues-rock band in the country, are the Fabulous Thunderbirds. The Thunderbirds (Jimmie Vaughan, Kim Wilson, Keith Ferguson, and Fran Christina) have dominated the Texas R and B scene since the mid-seventies. The distinctive guitar work of Jimmie Vaughan and the classic harmonica and vocals of Kim Wilson lay to rest forever such naive observations as "white boys can't play the blues."

The most promising blues performer of the 1980s was also a product of Austin and brother of the Thunderbirds' Jimmie Vaughan—guitar wizard Stevie Ray Vaughan. Vaughan was a veteran of such Austin blues-rock groups as Storm, Blackbird, and the Cobras. After the critical success of his 1983 album, *Texas Flood*, Stevie Ray Vaughan and his band Double Trouble (Chris Layton and Tommy Shannon) rapidly emerged as national stars. Vaughan's flair and raw talent—no one makes the guitar sing like Stevie Ray—rank him among the finest guitarists in the rich Texas R and B tradition.

Joining the Fabulous Thunderbirds and Stevie Ray Vaughan are quality blues performers like Paul Ray—one of the first Texas rockers to experiment with the blues back

in the sixties. Paul Ray and the Cobras rivaled the Thunderbirds for several years as Austin's favorite band. Other members of the Austin R and B family include Extreme Heat, W. C. Clark, Major Burkes, Omar and the Howlers, George Underwood and Blues Groove, Lewis and the Legends, and Ernie Sky and the K-Tels (led by Ernie Gammage). And there is a threesome of Austin women each one as good as any vocalist in America: Angela Strehli, Marcia Ball, and Lou Ann Barton — three emotion-laden voices that get better with every performance.

The Austin fascination with rhythm and blues is symbolic of the cyclical nature of Texas musical tastes. Many Texas musicians have returned to the roots that gave birth to jazz and rock 'n' roll. Only in this cycle, the blues originate in the city, and there is no color line to restrict performer or audience. Once again, the musicians are far more progressive than society at large — destroying the stereotypes and racial barriers that have limited our exposure to all the emotion and excitement of the blues experience. Those who cling to the old clichés cling to a racist past. It is a past that can be valued for its artistic and creative contributions, but a past that must be condemned for its repression of black music and for its denial of the dignity of the culture that nurtured it. Today's celebration of rhythm and blues promotes the promise and the spirit of a truly integrated society, both socially and musically.

♫

Janis. *(Texas Music Collection.)*

8
Rock 'n' Roll

That'll be the day, when you say good-bye

That'll be the day, when you say good-bye,
That'll be the day, when you make me cry,
You say you're gonna leave, you know it's a lie,
Cause that'll be the day when I die.

That'll Be the Day
Buddy Holly, Norman Petty, Jerry Allison

Rock 'n' roll was a child of the fifties. It was born into a post-war America whose identity was characterized by flat-top haircuts, backyard bomb shelters, and a naive national assumption that things would never change. But "the times they were a-changin'," and rock 'n' roll was the most visible symbol of that change to challenge America's innocence. It was music for the young—an irreverent sound that evoked sensuality, emotion, and a constant message from its converts that it "feels good." Rock was the only passion in a culture dominated by conformity and apathy.

There was nothing particularly original about the musical structure of rock 'n' roll. Its rhythmic lyrics and hard-driving beat were a result of the musical integration between blacks and whites in the American South. During the 1930s the roots of rock 'n' roll were already spreading—from the blues and jazz boogie clubs that dotted the Mississippi to the western-swing dance halls proliferating in Texas. In fact, most black Americans had been rock 'n' rolling for some twenty years before disc jockey Allan Freed gave it a label in the early fifties. And therein lies one of the reasons why the history of rock 'n' roll transcends music; it played a pivotal role in the sociological, and even political, development of America in the fifties and sixties. When the youth of America embraced the "wild, undignified noise" that had

grown out of black culture, white America came face to face with its racist past. The young were shocked into a frenzy of excitement and celebration; the rest of America was simply shocked.

The sociological or cultural implications of rock music meant little to those who loved its incessant beat and pulsating rhythms. Rockers laughed when told by pop-arranger Mitch Miller that "rock is not music, it's a disease." And they felt no need for redemption when an Alabama minister proclaimed, "Rock and roll is a means of pulling the white man down to the level of the Negro. It is part of a plot to undermine the morale of the youth of our nation." In Texas numerous record burnings were sponsored by local school boards, and more than one Texas city council passed ordinances banning public performances of "this lascivious devil music." These attacks on rock 'n' roll, as well as its role as a political force in the 1960s, often overshadowed the music itself—a music that rejects the ideology and social significance that so many analysts ascribe to it.

The first giants of the rock era appeared during the mid-fifties in perhaps the purest merger of rhythm and blues with the southern country tradition. They were the Memphis-based rockabillies (Elvis Presley, Carl Perkins, Johnny Cash, Jerry Lee Lewis), and it was their style that set the standards in rock musical technique and image from 1954 until 1957. But out on the South Texas plains an heir to the rockabilly legacy was beginning a spectacular three-year career that proved to be as innovative and legendary as any in rock 'n' roll history. That brief, but brilliant, career belonged to Charles Hardin "Buddy" Holly.

Buddy Holly was born on 7 September 1936 in Lubbock, Texas. He died 3 February 1959 in a snow-covered field between Clear Lake and Mason City, Iowa. The events that transpired during the last three years of Holly's life proved to be one of the most important stories in the history of Texas, as well as the history of American popular music. The story began at Lubbock High School when Buddy formed his first rockabilly group with classmates Bob Montgomery and Larry Welborn. Known both as Buddy and Bob, and the Western and Bop Band, the group gained local acceptance on an area radio program, at school dances, and at the grand openings of several Lubbock businesses. Their first break came in October of 1955 when they opened a show for Bill Haley and the Comets at Lubbock's famed Cotton Club. The following night they opened for Elvis Presley. A recording contract with Decca soon followed, and Buddy and his new band, the Three Tunes (Jerry Allison, Sonny Curtis, and Don Guess), found themselves in Nashville. But Nashville was not ready for West Texas rock 'n' roll, and the recording session was a failure. Frustrated by the conservative musical heirarchy that ruled Nashville in the 1950s, the Texans returned home.

It took nearly twenty years for Nashville to realize that its future was tied to rock 'n' roll, and ironically, it was a contingent of Texans (this time from Austin) who made that point in the early seventies. But country music's loss was mainstream rock's gain, and back in Lubbock Buddy Holly was assembling one of rock 'n' roll's greatest bands, the Crickets. The Crickets (Jerry Allison, Niki Sullivan, Larry Welborn, and, later, Joe Mauldin) were the first white group to utilize the R and B format of lead guitar, rhythm guitar, bass, and drums. Buddy Holly's musical flair and direction and the Crickets' style and structure were the role model for the group-oriented rockers of the sixties, from the Beatles to the Doors to the Rolling Stones.

The career of Buddy Holly took off when he teamed with Clovis, New Mexico, producer and songwriter Norman Petty. Under Petty's guidance, Buddy achieved national prominence literally overnight. His first hit, *That'll Be the Day*, reached number three on the charts. The one-night stands and the hits continued for the next two years, with such rock classics as *Peggy Sue, Maybe Baby, Rave On, Everyday, True Love Ways, Raining in My Heart*, and *It Doesn't Matter Anymore*. On one of his tours in 1958 Buddy toured England, and in that audience were fans Eric Clapton, Paul McCartney, and John Lennon. All later remarked on the impact of that concert, and they obviously grasped the significance of the fact that Holly was the first white rock performer to write most of his material.

During the last months of his life Buddy and his new bride moved to New York, and he began to experiment with a complex variety of musical styles. He never abandoned his rockabilly roots, but he added strings and sometimes even full orchestration. Often described as rock's original "soft rocker," Holly was expanding the definition of rock 'n' roll and openly displaying its similarity to rhythm and blues, as well as to the Tex-Mex sounds of the Southwest. The

Johnny Preston (center) being interviewed by producer Huey Meaux. Preston had one of 1959's major hits, *Running Bear*. (*Huey Meaux Collection.*)

Roy Orbison in a scene from the movie *The Fastest Guitar Alive*. (*Texas Music Collection.*)

Buddy Holly in performance, 1958. *(Courtesy of Bill Griggs, Buddy Holly Memorial Society.)*

measure of an artist's creativity and genius can be witnessed by his or her staying power, and in that regard, the Buddy Holly legacy gets stronger as musical styles get more diverse.

In January of 1959, Buddy joined the Winter Dance Party tour featuring Ritchie Valens, Dion and the Belmonts, and the "Big Bopper" (J. P. Richardson). "Jape" Richardson, a former disc jockey from Beaumont, had just scored a giant hit with *Chantilly Lace.* Buddy's band at the time consisted of Tommy Allsup on guitar, Charlie Bunch on drums, and a young bass player from Littlefield, Texas, named Waylon Jennings. After a performance in Clear Lake, Iowa, Buddy chartered a plane to fly him and his band to the next stop on the tour. The Big Bopper convinced Waylon Jennings to give up his seat, and Ritchie Valens replaced Tommy Allsup. Just after midnight on 3 February 1959 the plane went down. In the words of folk-rocker Don McLean's 1971 epic, *American Pie,* that was "the day the music died." And in fact, it was the end of an exciting era for rock. It would be another five years before four Englishmen infused American popular music with a style that rivaled the fresh and experimental directions taken by Buddy Holly.

Rock 'n' roll had no real identity in the years between Buddy Holly's death and the arrival of the Beatles. There were scores of teen idols on the scene, but most of the pop songs on the charts claiming to be rock 'n' roll had little of the raw vitality of Holly or the other rock innovators like Chuck Berry. Elvis had abandoned his roots and "gone Hollywood," and many of the rockabillies had "gone Nashville." But one of the Memphis rockabillies became a dominant figure in those years when rock was struggling with its own image. He was the most successful singer and songwriter of rock ballads in the early sixties, Roy Orbison—another one of the long line of rockers who played their licks against the winds of West Texas.

Roy Orbison began his professional music career as an eight-year-old country singer. By the time he formed the Wink Westerners at Wink High School, his repertoire ranged from pure hillbilly to pop hits and Big Band swing. Orbison's first break came while he was attending North Texas State University. He played backup on the initial recording effort of another NTSU student, Pat Boone. That led to a recording opportunity of his own at Norman Petty's Clovis studio, and from that session came *Ooby Dooby,* a moderate hit for Orbison and his new band, the Teen-Kings. The success with Petty led to a short-lived contract with Sun Records in Memphis and eventually to a more enduring relationship with Monument Records in Nashville. After his first million seller, *Only the Lonely,* the hits penned and sung

Waylon and Buddy. *(Courtesy of Bill Griggs, Buddy Holly Memorial Society.)*

Carolyn Hester was the leader of the folk scene at the University of Texas in the early sixties and later went on to national fame as Texas' finest folksinger. *(Doug Hanners Collection.)*

The Sir Douglas Quintet. *(Huey Meaux Collection.)*

Rock 'n' roll, Texas Panhandle-style—the Cinders (left to right: J. D. Souther, Charlie Bates, and Steve Dodge). *(Courtesy of Charlie Bates.)*

by Roy Orbison consistently achieved commercial and critical success in the rock world from 1960 until 1964: *Running Scared, Crying, Dream Baby, It's Over, Candy Man, Mean Woman Blues, Blue Bayou,* and *Pretty Woman.* The loss of his family in two tragic accidents, as well as the British invasion of rock, slowed Orbison's career in the 1960s. But a momentum began to build in the seventies when a new generation discovered and rerecorded his songs, and his career was revived. He had a giant hit on the country charts in 1980 in a duet with Emmylou Harris, *That Lovin' You Feeling Again.* Before his untimely death in 1988, Orbison triumphed again with success as a member of the Travelin' Wilburys.

Buddy Holly and Roy Orbison were Texas' major contribution to rock 'n' roll in its first ten years. However, there were an enormous number of rock bands sprouting all over the state—rockabillies like Ray Campi, Mac Curtis, Billy Dee, Johnny Carroll, Ray Ruff, Gene Summers, and Sid King. Johnny Preston from Port Arthur had a number-one hit in 1959 with his *Running Bear.* Ray Peterson of Denton had two national successes in 1960 with *Corinna, Corinna* and *Tell Laura I Love Her. Hey! Baby* by Bruce Channel of Grapevine was one of the biggest hits in the nation in

Knox and the Rhythm Orchids. The Knox-Bowen duo wrote two songs that made it to the national charts, *Party Doll* and *I'm Stickin' with You.* Bowen later went into production and is now president of Warner Brothers Records in Nashville. Fifteen miles up the road, in Amarillo, another group followed the example of local heroes Buddy Holly, Buddy Knox, and Jimmy Bowen. Part of Norman Petty's Clovis productions, they were Jimmy Gilmer and the Fireballs (George Tomsco, Stan Lark, Eric Budd). The Fireballs were the most popular dance band in the area for several years, and in 1963 they had one of the year's biggest hits, *Sugar Shack.*

At the other end of the state, Texas' most prolific producer was grinding out a blend of Tex-Mex and Cajun rock, first from his barbershop in Winnie, and later from studios in Houston and San Antonio. He was Huey Meaux, affectionately known by his friends as "the Crazy Cajun." Hits on his labels included Sunny and the Sunliners' *Talk to Me,* Roy Head with *Treat Her Right,* Barbara Lynn with *You'll Lose a Good Thing,* Jivin' Gene and the Jokers with *Breaking Up Is Hard to Do,* Joe Barry's *I'm a Fool to Care,* and several hits by Dale and Grace. Through the mid-sixties and into the seventies Meaux had continued prosperity with such performers as Doug Sahm (Sir Douglas Quintet), B. J. Thomas, and Freddy Fender.

Only known as one of the Monkees by most of the public, Michael Nesmith has been a pioneer in country-rock, an innovator in music video, and the composer of some of rock's most poignant and prophetic lyrics: "The straight folks think that winning gives them license to kill, But number good is better than number one." *(Courtesy of the Pacific Arts Corporation.)*

1962. Major Bill Smith in Fort Worth was producing Channel along with a young rockabilly named Delbert McClinton, the leader of the Rondels. Smith produced the Rondels' best-seller, *If You Really Want Me To I'll Go,* and J. Frank Wilson's *Last Kiss.* He also produced a 1963 hit for a couple of Howard Payne University students, Ray Hildebrand and Jill Jackson. Their hit was *Hey, Paul;* their recording name was Paul and Paula. Texas boogie-rock star Ray Sharpe similarly came out of the Fort Worth scene with his rock-classic *Linda Lu.* With a steady stream of hits for four years, Major Bill was the dominant Texas producer of pop-rock during the early sixties.

Instrumentals were extremely popular in the late fifties and early sixties. One of the biggest instrumentals of the era was *Tequila,* a hard-rocking Tex-Mex song by the Champs. Two of the Champs were Texans, Jim Seals from Sidney and Dash Crofts from Cisco. They started their careers in Cisco with a band called Dean Beard and the Crew Cats. After leaving the Champs, they had moderate success with the Mushrooms and the Dawnbreakers. In the 1970s Seals and Crofts emerged as one of the most popular exponents of soft rock.

In the Panhandle, two groups had a small dose of national exposure and success. Buddy Knox from Canyon and Jimmy Bowen from Dumas joined with West Texas State University friends Don Lanier and Dave Allred to form Buddy

B. J. Thomas has had success on both the rock and country charts for nearly two decades. *(Rick Henson.)*

The Five Americans. (*Doug Hanners Collection.*)

Kenneth Threadgill and Janis Joplin. Janis began her career at Threadgill's in Austin singing country and blues. This photo was taken three months before her death in October of 1970. (*David Gahr, courtesy of Kenneth Threadgill Collection.*)

Janis during her first year in Austin. (*Kenneth Threadgill Collection.*)

From 1959 to 1964, rock music came under increasingly severe criticism. It was seen as devoid of originality, seriousness, or even quality, and much of that was an accurate indictment. Characterized as pablum for a generation unaware of the social chaos unfolding around it, rock was now a major industry, and many critics viewed it as a perpetrator of the corporate mentality that ignored racism, repression, and militarism. However, on the college campuses, a folk revival was brewing in the late fifties which eventually would merge with rock 'n' roll. It was a revival of the spirit of Woody Guthrie; and it moved rock into the political arena of the 1960s.

At first the folk craze rejected commercialism, but as the successful artists soon found out, it became increasingly difficult to sing of poverty and struggle when your bank balance hit six figures. Despite the ironies and contradictions in its message, folk and folk-rock changed American society more, and in a shorter period of time, than any single person or phenomenon in American social history. Within a few short years, Middle-America's youth were demanding that society adhere to the lyrics that they had learned from their music. The success of the civil rights movement and the end of a war in Asia owe much to the message of the folk song and the emotional power of rock 'n' roll.

Texas society felt the changes also. However, the folk movement in Texas, as well as the corresponding social activism, was isolated in the larger cities and on a few college campuses. Most Texas musicians migrated to California or New York to escape the social and political conservatism prevalent in the state. Some of those Texans whose careers began in the folk field emerged as the super stars of the 1970s. One member of a folk group, the Chad Mitchell Trio, was a former Texas Tech student who had grown up in Fort Worth. His name was John Deutschendorf, better known as John Denver. The lead singer for the New Christy Minstrels, perhaps the most successful of the folk groups in the mid-sixties, was Houston-born Kenny Rogers. Another folk

Stephen Stills, 1981. *(Scott Newton.)*

group that had a string of hits was the Pozo-Seco Singers. Their leader was Don Williams from Portland, Texas — one of the major forces in country music through the seventies and eighties. Several other Texans made their mark in the folk era as single performers. Trini López from Dallas had one of 1963's most influential recordings, *If I Had a Hammer*. Lopez had a thriving career during the sixties, combining folk lyrics with a Latin-based rock rhythm. And during the folk boom of the early sixties, Texas' greatest female folk artist, Carolyn Hester, enjoyed tremendous success in California and New York. Originally from Waco, Hester was the queen of Austin's early folk scene. Her voice is still as vibrant and her message just as inspirational every spring when she headlines the Kerrville Folk Festival.

Just as the folk-rock era restructured the American political spectrum, the arrival of the Beatles in 1964 dramatically altered America's social institutions. It was the beginning of a cultural renaissance that challenged American hypocrisy, self-righteousness, and materialism. For the music industry it meant new directions, and one of the first producers in the country to realize that was Huey Meaux. Meaux gathered together a group of San Antonio Tex-Mex musicians, had them grow their hair to Beatle specifications, gave them an English name, and promptly delivered a major hit, *She's About a Mover*. The group was the Sir Douglas Quintet (Doug Sahm, Augie Meyers, Jack Barber, John Pérez, Frank Morin, and later, Rocky Morales). The band worked out of San Francisco during the sixties, and they had a number of successful albums in addition to the follow-up hit, *Mendocino*. In the seventies the Quintet returned to Texas where Sahm and Meyers both took part in the

development of the Austin sound. There is no musician who more effectively symbolizes Texas music than Doug Sahm. He is proficient in producing quality rock, country, rhythm and blues, Cajun, or Tex-Mex. His versatility is unmatched by any American musican.

Another response to the British invasion was the television-inspired rock group, the Monkees. One of the members of that manufactured quartet was Texan Michael Nesmith. Nesmith was the most accomplished musician in the Monkees, and he was the only one whose musical career continued after the group's demise in 1968. Nesmith grew up in Dallas and became a regular on the folk club circuit while attending college in San Antonio. After a move to California, he wrote and performed in the Los Angeles area before landing a role with the Monkees. His talent was recognized by other musicians, if not by the public, and one of his songs, *Different Drum*, was a moderate hit for Linda Ronstadt and the Stone Poneys. During the 1970s Nesmith and his First National Band had a substantial following in country-rock with notable records like *Joanne, Silver Moon*, and *Harmony Constant*. Nesmith was a pioneer in the development and marketing of video discs, and in fact, he won the first Grammy given for videos with *Elephant Parts*, featuring his hit single *Rio*.

As trends and tastes became more complex in the rock world of the mid- and late sixties, Texans played an increasingly visible role. Dallas-born Sylvester Stewart, leader of Sly and the Family Stone, had giant hits with *Everday People, Hot Fun in the Summertime*, and *I Want to Take You Higher*. Kenny Rogers, born in Houston and raised in

89

Crockett, moved from folk to rock with the First Edition. Producer Huey Meaux developed another star performer in B. J. Thomas (known for his renditions of *I'm So Lonesome I Could Cry* and *Raindrops Keep Falling on My Head*). Shawn Phillips emerged as a leader of the continuing folk-rock sound. Sam the Sham (Domingo Samudio) and the Pharaohs scored a novelty hit with *Woolly Bully*. The Bobby Fuller Four put El Paso on the musical map with their successful single, *I Fought the Law*. The Dallas-based Five Americans had two successful releases, *Western Union* and *I Saw the Light*. Dobie Gray from Houston had hits with *The In Crowd, Loving Arms*, and *Drift Away*. And one of rock's most influential figures appeared on the California scene in 1966, Dallas native Stephen Stills. As a member of the group Buffalo Springfield, he wrote and sang one of the sixties most eloquent statements on the protest movement and the social dynamics that were dividing America. Like the youth movement it mirrored, *For What It's Worth* told the establishment that it not only had the wrong answers, it was asking the wrong questions. Stills, of course, became part of the super-group Crosby, Stills, Nash, and Young. A few of his classic songs include *Suite: Judy Blue Eyes, Love the One You're With, 4+20, Carry On*, and *Dark Star*. The creative and commercial career of Stephen Stills is still thriving into the 1980s.

Musicians, their audiences, and American society itself were caught in a frenzied pace of turmoil and change during the last three years of the sixties. Political assassinations, urban riots, an endless war, and acid rock—they all blended together; reality had become a hallucination. One performer lived that "bad trip" and symbolized the contradiction of having to be liberated in a free society. She was proclaimed the best white blues singer in American musical history—rock 'n' roll's greatest female star—the personification of the sixties generation. She was all of these, but Janis Joplin was also a lonely, tragic young woman from a small town in Texas.

Growing up in Protestant Texas during the 1950s produced a great number of victims, but none was as visible or as vocal as Janis Joplin. Born in Port Arthur in 1943, Janis suffered our society's severest form of discrimination as a young teenager—she was unpopular. She had plain features, a trace of acne, a weight problem, and nondescript hair that refused to follow the bouffant styles of the day. The ostracism she felt as a youth was a curse that Janis carried with her to her death in 1970, and it was obviously a factor in the flamboyant and defiant image that became her trademark.

Janis left Port Arthur in the summer of 1962 and moved to Austin. She believed that the environment at the University of Texas would be different; she was wrong. The fraternity-sorority complex dominated the campus, and conservatism and conformity ruled the future social oasis of Texas. Janis lived on the fringe of university life with "the folkies" who set up residence at UT's Union Building as if it were their own Greenwich Village. On her arrival, Janis joined Powell St. John (later of Mother Earth fame) and Lanny Wiggins to form the Waller Creek Boys. They sang folk, bluegrass, a little country, and a lot of blues. The Waller Creek Boys were regulars at the UT Union and a refurbished old gas station named Threadgill's. Its owner was Austin's resident yodeler and country music legend, Kenneth Threadgill. Threadgill befriended Janis at their first meeting, and

Tracy Nelson backstage at the Vulcan Gas Company, 1969. *(Burton Wilson.)*

he was one of the few people whom she always referred to with genuine affection.

Janis left Austin in 1963 and followed friends to the promised land of San Francisco. No doubt she was hurt and bitter at the time—she had just been nominated by some fraternity boys for the Ugliest Man on Campus Award. Settling in at the North Beach area of San Francisco, Janis surrounded herself with artists and musicians. It was apparently a happy and exciting period for her; there is little need to rebel when you live among the rebellious. She sang in a variety of small clubs in the Bay area, usually a cappella or with only a guitar accompaniment. For the next two years Janis moved back and forth between New York and San Francisco, drinking heavily and experimenting with any new drug that appeared on the scene. The speed finally took its toll, and the eighty-five-pound, confused young woman returned to Texas.

Soon Janis was back in Austin performing at the folk-rock club, The Eleventh Door. At that time she was seriously considering joining Austin's, and indeed Texas', premier rock group, the Thirteenth Floor Elevators. But the lure of San Francisco's psychedelic era led Janis back to the Haight-Ashbury district, and within months, she

Roky Erickson, leader of the Thirteenth Floor Elevators, the first psychedelic band. *(Scott Newton.)*

Johnny Winter. *(Burton Wilson.)*

Shiva's Headband at a "love-in" in Austin, 1969. *(Burton Wilson.)*

Edgar Winter. *(Courtesy of CBS Records.)*

became the queen of acid rock. Her musical rise began when she joined a local San Francisco group, Big Brother and the Holding Company. Their performance at the Monterey Pop Festival in 1967 brought Janis national acclaim. Her bluesy growls, screaming lyrics, and frantic stage presence were unbelievable to the critical San Francisco crowd. They had never seen a woman, or at least a white woman, sing rock 'n' roll the way Janis sang it. The Monterey Festival led to a major nationally acclaimed album for Big Brother and Janis, *Cheap Thrills.* Two hit singles came from the album, *Piece of My Heart* and *Ball and Chain.* Following a split with Big Brother and the Holding Company in 1968, Janis released her first solo album, *I Got Dem Ol' Kozmic Blues Again, Mama.* She was now a genuine superstar in the world of rock 'n' roll.

The fame and the money were never enough for Janis Joplin. As she achieved her greatest success, the loneliness that had plagued her most of her life became an obsession. She often remarked, "Every night I make love to twenty-five thousand people onstage, but I go home alone." The drugs that had become her closest companions finally took her life on 4 October, 1970. The coroner's report ruled death due to an accidental overdose of morphine derivatives and alcohol. Soon after her death, the *Pearl* album was released; that album, which included Janis' version of the Kris Kristofferson song *Me and Bobby McGee,* was one of the biggest-selling albums in history.

The life of Janis Joplin has continually been viewed as symbolic of many of America's social ills. Some see her as a victim of a sexually repressive society; others see her as another woman casualty of trying to achieve in a man's world. But sociological analysis only trivializes her life. She was a musician—a dynamic human being. That alone is enough to grant her the respect in death that she rarely received in her short but creative life.

Janis Joplin's meteoric rise to superstardom and her turbulent lifestyle overshadowed the accomplishments of many other Texas rock artists at the time. But a great number of Texans were achieving national renown playing hard psychedelic rock and experimental jazz-rock, as well as the more polished, smoother songs that came to be known as the "California sound." One of the favorite San Francisco bands of the psychedelic period was the Texas group Mother Earth. Led by Tracy Nelson and Powell St. John, they were basically a rhythm and blues band, but their style was defined by all the trappings of acid rock. Watching Mother Earth rock through a light show at The Fillmore was made even more unforgettable by the powerful vocal delivery of Tracy Nelson. It matters little if she sings blues, country, or rock; no one in music has a more distinctive, emotion-packed voice.

On the other coast, a couple of brothers from Beaumont were enjoying the rock critics' raves. Johnny Winter made the break from Texas first, but he was soon followed by brother Edgar. Both had been influenced heavily by the black musical heritage that thrived in the working-class sections of Southeast Texas. New York audiences loved the electric blues and electric jazz produced by the Winters' guitars and keyboards. Johnny and Edgar Winter usually worked separately, except for an occasional tour and two joint albums, most notably *Together: Edgar and Johnny Winter.* Throughout the seventies the Winter brothers branched out into a variety of rhythm and blues and jazz-oriented directions, but both also appear to have moved back to their rock 'n' roll roots on their latest efforts.

Texas had a great many regional bands that provided quality rock 'n' roll during the late sixties and into the seventies. Prominent among that group were Shiva's Headband, Kenny and the Kasuals, Bad Seeds, Bubble Puppy, Red Krayola, the Chessman, the Five Americans, Fever Tree, American Blues, Moving Sidewalks, the Briks, Conqueroo, and the Thirteenth Floor Elevators. The Elevators, led by Roky Erickson, were rock's first psychedelic band, and from their Austin base in the mid-sixties they had a national hit with *You're Gonna Miss Me.* In the words of music historian Doug Hanners, the legendary Elevators were "acidized country boys playing psychedelic Buddy Holly riffs." Another regional group from Texas that kept getting more and more national exposure before finally emerg-

Jim Seals and Dash Crofts. *(Courtesy of Warner Brothers Records.)*

England Dan and John Ford Coley had several hits in the mid-seventies, when soft rock dominated the charts. Dan Seals is the brother of Jim Seals of Seals and Crofts. *(Scott Newton.)*

Christopher Cross played in local dance bands in Austin and San Antonio before achieving national fame. *(Photo by Matthew Rolston, courtesy of Warner Brothers Records.)*

ZZ Top, 1981. *(Courtesy Warner Brothers Records.)*

J. D. Souther. *(Courtesy of Frontline Management.)*

ing as major stars was "that little ol' band from Texas," ZZ Top. Composed of guitarist Billy Gibbons, bassist Dusty Hill, and drummer Frank Beard, ZZ Top was Texas' most successful rock group of the seventies. From their first album in 1971 to their 1983 album, *Eliminator,* they have had a string of platinum albums including *Tres Hombres, Fandango, Tejas, El Loco,* and *Deguello.* ZZ Top's Texas caricature and western imagery cannot disguise these hard-metal rockers whose innovative lyrics and high decibel level have come to symbolize the epitome of Texas rock 'n' roll.

Rock music and America's turbulent social climate were both tempered by the 1970s. Rock 'n' roll bore no resemblance to the conformity-shattering and establishment-threatening sound of its early years. It was now part of the capitalist establishment — a giant corporate industry that no longer challenged the society from which it sprang or the financiers who paid its bills. Two distinct styles dominated rock directions during the 1970s, up-tempo, pop-oriented disco and the so-called mellow rock emanating from California. The leaders of the California sound, the Eagles, had a very definite Texas influence. One of their members, Don Henley, was from Gilmer, a small town deep in the forests of Northeast Texas. Henley was originally a drummer in his high school band, Shiloh, before he ended up in California with a record contract. His first California group went nowhere, but in 1971 Henley joined forces with Glenn Frey and Randy Meisner to back up Linda Ronstadt. After they were joined by Bernie Leadon, the Eagles released their first hit in June of 1972, *Take It Easy.* That began a string of hit singles and albums unrivaled by any performers during the next decade. Among the many songs coauthored by Henley and his fellow Eagles are *Best of My Love, Take It to the Limit, Tequila Sunrise, Lyin' Eyes, Desperado,* and *Hotel California.*

Another Texan whose career is linked with the Eagles and the rest of the "California mafia" of soft rockers is J. D. Souther from Amarillo. Souther's career began in the Texas Panhandle in the early sixties with a regional band called the Cinders (Souther on drums and vocals, Charlie Bates on rhythm guitar and vocals, and Steve Dodge on lead guitar). After moving to California, Souther teamed with future

Boz Scaggs, backstage at the Armadillo in Austin, 1972. *(Burton Wilson.)*

Meat Loaf—his *Bat Out of Hell* album has been one of the biggest sellers in rock 'n' roll history. *(Courtesy of Epic Records.)*

Eagle, Glenn Frey, to form Longbranch Pennywhistle. That association brought about one album, but it also thrust Souther into a partnership and friendship with Linda Ronstadt, Jackson Browne, and the rest of the Eagles. Souther co-wrote several of the Eagle hits, such as *Best of My Love, New Kid in Town, James Dean,* and *Doolin-Dalton.* In addition to producing for Linda Ronstadt, he wrote and also sang on such Ronstadt tunes as *Don't Cry Now* and *Faithless Love.* J. D. Souther was part of the Souther-Hillman-Furay Band in the mid-seventies, but his greatest success came with the release of his hit single, *You're Only Lonely,* in 1980.

Other Texans made substantial contributions to the soft rock craze, or "pop and roll," as it was often labeled. After their stint with the Champs and several other groups in the sixties, Jim Seals and Dash Crofts received a phenomenal reception as a duo in 1972 with the release of *Summer Breeze.* Another platinum album, *Diamond Girl,* followed the next year. Johnny Nash of Houston also gained a national reputation at the time with his reggae-rock version of *I Can See Clearly Now.* And, one of the most promising Texas rock stars, Meat Loaf (alias Marvin Aday from Dallas) burst upon the scene in the late seventies. Billy Preston, born in Dallas, was now parlaying his association with the Beatles into a career embracing jazz, rhythm and blues, and soft-rock ballads. One of the rock world's most intelligent, if not eclectic, sounds of the seventies emanated from Fort Worth native T-Bone Burnett. By the end of the decade, Christopher Cross was the undisputed leader of soft rock. Originally from San Antonio, Cross moved to Austin in the early seventies and made a living playing at fraternity dances and small clubs. After signing with Warner Brothers Records in 1978, the *Christopher Cross* album was released. With singles like *Sailing, Never Be the Same,* and *Ride Like the Wind,* Cross swept the 1981 Grammy Awards with five Grammy Awards. He followed that up the next year with another Grammy for the *Theme from Arthur.*

Two Texas rock 'n' rollers whose careers have spanned two decades are still performing, writing, innovating, and selling records. They are old schoolmates from the suburbs of North Dallas, Boz Scaggs and Steve Miller. From their first group, the Marksmen, to their solo careers through the seventies and eighties, Scaggs and Miller have proved to be two of rock's most durable, if not successful, artists. William Royce "Boz" Scaggs was always a critic's choice during the 1960s, but his rhythm-and-blues rock was not particularly commercial at the time. But by the mid-seventies the disco dance beat was ruling the charts and Scaggs was suddenly in style. His *Silk Degrees* album yielded such singles as *Lowdown* and *Lido Shuffle.* The pure, melodic voice of Boz Scaggs and his continually evolving style have kept him high on the pop-rock charts as he enters his third decade of rock 'n' roll.

The list of Steve Miller hits is an impressive one: *Living in the U.S.A., Space Cowboy, Gangster of Love, The Joker, Take the Money and Run, Jet Airliner, Fly Like an Eagle,* and his most recent, *Abracadabra.* No Texas rock performer has had the consistent success of album sales and concert tours of Steve Miller. His music has evolved from the late sixties performances of blues-rock at San Francisco's Avalon Ballroom to a mass appeal brand of middle-of-the-road rock 'n' roll. Whatever formula he follows, Steve Miller continues to outlive the critics who claim he only gives the public what they want, perhaps for an obvious reason—the music is good.

Steve Miller, 1977. *(Scott Newton.)*

The current Texas rock scene, as well as its future development, owes a great debt to the diverse musical resurgence that occurred in Austin during the seventies. There are no longer any restrictions defining musical direction or style. Most so-called country bands now play hard rock riffs as standard segments of their performance. The new wave bands incorporate country stylings and rockabilly with equal ease. And all of the Texas bands today acknowledge their debt to the rhythm and blues tradition that is the backbone of American popular music. Those who charge that rock has lost its cutting edge and its vitality ignore the reality of today's Texas music, or they get their rock from the commercially restricted dead airwaves of modern radio. If you want to hear the best of rock 'n' roll—the mass folk art of the twentieth century—it can be found in the clubs and concert halls of America's capital of live music, Austin, Texas. There the Texas tradition of Buddy Holly and Janis Joplin continues to live and grow.

♫

Willie Nelson — the most successful artist and influential personality in the history of Texas music. (*Rick Henson.*)

9

Modern Country

Turn out the lights, the party's over

Turn out the lights, the party's over,
They say that all good things must end.
Let's call it a night, the party's over,
And tomorrow start the same old
thing again.

The Party's Over
Willie Nelson

Country music, as an artistic and a commercial entity, was searching for its own identity in the mid-1950s following the steady drift from its southeastern folk roots that began with the tragic death of Hank Williams in 1953. And of course, the onslaught of competition from rock 'n' roll and the changing cultural tastes of American society also posed a challenge to the unique rural styles and traditions that constituted the country sound. Post–World War II America was fascinated with the new technology of the era and the increased urbanization that it brought. Suburbia was in vogue—the simpler, rural message revered by country music was viewed as unsophisticated and provincial by much of the new, affluent middle class. To combat the threat of extinction, country producers and performers broadened their base by expanding styles and instrumentation and by modifying the rural lyrics. They merged country and pop—the "Nashville Sound" was born.

The country-pop alliance of the late fifties and early sixties increased corporate profits and brought national visibility to country artists, but it also threatened the country music purists. And in fact, the success of the Nashville formula lay in its use of skilled studio musicians and professionally produced and promoted material that appealed to urban and non-southern audiences. Many critics of the new directions

lamented the rejection of traditional instruments (fiddles, steel guitars, and the basic country instrument, a high-pitched nasal voice) and the obvious concession to the youth-oriented rock influences. But country-pop rejuvenated a dying industry and preserved a recording base for those who were not willing to abandon their allegiance to the purer country heritage.

The most graphic example of that allegiance was a young singer from Saratoga, Texas. He has been labeled the "country singer's singer" and "the world's greatest country performer;" George Jones is the industry's most prolific and successful personality of the last twenty-five years. Of all the Texans in Nashville, Jones has remained closest to his honky-tonk roots and the early southern country styles.

George Jones grew up in the newly industrialized area surrounding Beaumont and Port Arthur. His family was rural in attitudes and values and southern in their working-class fundamentalism. They were representative of the rural lifestyle thrust into the urban world, and it was just such a mixture that created the honky-tonk tradition. Jones has never lost touch with the hard country sound that he learned listening to the jukeboxes that served the refineries and factories of Southeast Texas.

George Jones in the 1950s, at the beginning of one of Nashville's most illustrious careers. *(Leon and Chic Carter.)*

Roger Miller began the country crossover to pop in the mid-1960s. *(Rick Henson.)*

Johnny Gimble (left) and George Jones, 1982. *(Rick Henson.)*

Jones started his career in Beaumont with Starday Records in 1954. The founders of Starday, H.W. "Pappy" Dailey and Jack Starnes, moved with George Jones to Nashville after his 1955 hit *Why Baby Why*. In 1962, Jones hit the top of the country charts with *She Thinks I Still Care*. It was the number-one record of the year and brought Jones various awards as country music's singer of the year. Throughout the sixties the career of George Jones had its highs (hits such as *Take Me, Walk through This World with Me, Just One More, White Lightning, The Window Up Above*, and *Don't Stop the Music*), and it also had its lows as Jones battled an alcohol problem. His career was revitalized in 1969 following his marriage to Tammy Wynette and their subsequent series of duet albums. That partnership ended in divorce in 1975, but neither career suffered. Jones' string of hits continued in the seventies with *The Grand Tour, Ragged but Right*, and culminated in 1981 with the biggest country record of the young decade, *He Stopped Lovin' Her Today*.

The George Jones style is unmistakable—a tenor wail that blends perfectly with steel guitar and fiddle. His emotional phrasing and East Texas twang are pure country. With over 150 albums to his credit, George Jones remains the dominant performer in today's Nashville establishment.

A number of Texans rivaled Jones for country music supremacy during the early sixties. One of those was Sherman-born Alvis Edgar "Buck" Owens. Although Owens grew up in Arizona and perfected his musical skill in California, his distinctive style (a nasal twang in his voice and a reliance on the pedal-steel guitar) was immediately recognizable as part of the Texas honky-tonk school. Another Texan, Jimmy Dean of Plainview, was country music's most visible, and probably most famous performer from 1962 until 1965. Even though Dean had only one hit record, *Big Bad John*, he embodied country music for most Americans because of his television exposure. He hosted a morning program on CBS for several years, and then in 1964 he emceed a one-hour country music show in prime time for ABC. Dean and his television program were essentially country-pop and were forerunners of the crossover trend that became the standard in the 1970s.

The most successful proponent of country crossover in

the 1960s was an inventive songwriter-singer who dominated the 1965 Grammy Awards, Roger Miller. His six Grammy victories are still an unprecedented achievement. Miller was born in Fort Worth and spent his youth in various small Oklahoma and Texas towns. At one time he played with Ray Price's Cherokee Cowboys and wrote songs for both Price and George Jones. It was Miller's songwriting ability that brought him fame with such classics as *King of the Road, Dang Me, Husbands and Wives, I've Been a Long Time Leavin'*, and *England Swings.* Nashville had never seen lyrics with such wit and originality, and as a result the country music heirarchy began to acknowledge that country audiences wanted more than songs about drinking or lost love. Miller's recent career appears to have been revitalized with his 1983 hit *Old Friends*, a tribute to those who shared his love of and struggles within the music industry. Singing with him on that recording are Miller's old friends Ray Price and Willie Nelson. Roger Miller brought an intelligence and a spirit to Nashville that ushered in a new era — an era in which two other Texans revolutionized country music.

The lives and careers of these two singer-songwriters changed the direction and imagery of Nashville music, helped merge the country sound with rock, united the rural and urban audiences, and brought a new genius and imagination to American popular music. They are two close friends who have taken country music to new creative heights, Willie Nelson and Kris Kristofferson.

Kris Kristofferson in concert. *(Photo by Scott Newton, courtesy of "Austin City Limits".)*

Kris Kristofferson changed the course of country music in the early 1970s. His songs were a brilliant combination of sensitivity, honesty, and symbolism. *(Rick Henson.)*

Willie Nelson at Big G's Club in Round Rock, 1973. *(Scott Newton.)*

Mickey Raphael, harmonica wizard with the Willie Nelson Band. *(Rick Henson.)*

Nelson and Kristofferson were the catalysts for a clash of cultures in the world of country music during the early 1970s. The Nashville establishment, a group of record company executives and performers, felt that it represented country music and therefore had control over its content. Some of these "Opryland gentry" were country purists and some were advocates of country-pop. The clash came when a new generation of performers challenged both groups with their independence, their appearance, their lifestyle, and especially, with their musical diversity. The press labeled them outlaws or Nashville rebels. Writer Dave Hickey describes the conflict of interests between the old guard and the new in his observation that "the rebels are just about the only folks in Nashville who will walk into a room where there's a guitar and a *Wall Street Journal* and pick up the guitar." The leader of that new generation of writers and singers was Kris Kristofferson.

The life of Kris Kristofferson reads like a verse from one of his songs, *The Pilgrim: Chapter 33:*

> **He's a poet, he's a picker;**
> **He's a prophet, he's a pusher;**
> **He's a pilgrim and a preacher and a**
> **problem when he's stoned;**
> **He's a walking contradiction;**
> **Partly truth and partly fiction**
> **Takin' every wrong direction on his**
> **lonely way back home.**

And indeed, the contradictions are obvious. He was a Rhodes' Scholar, and later a janitor in an RCA studio. He was a football player and boxer, but he wanted to write music. He was a helicopter pilot, and he sang in a country band. He was an army captain, yet he sang some of the most moving antiwar songs of the era. But eventually the truth and the fiction merged, and Kristofferson had hit after hit, which assured him a prominent role among the finest writers of American music.

Kristofferson's impact on Nashville emanated from several sources. He represented the changes, and therefore the challenges, facing the Nashville status quo. The new breed of songwriters openly defied the hypocrisy and racism that had long been a part of conservative Nashville. Kristofferson also brought an honesty and integrity to country music lyrics. His songs spoke of sexuality without guilt, drugs without condemnation, and alienation without despair. Kristofferson's style was traditional country in many respects, but the imagery and introspection of his lyrics reached out and touched millions of young Americans who previously had rejected the reactionary political and social messages of country music.

The songs are classics: *Loving Her Was Easier Than Anything I'll Ever Do Again, Help Me Make It through the Night, For the Good Times, Jody and the Kid, The Taker, The Silver-Tongued Devil and I, Why Me, Sunday Mornin' Comin' Down,* and *Billy Dee.* And there was *Me and Bobby McGee,* a song that topped both country and rock charts (with Roger Miller and Janis Joplin doing respective versions) and whose message became an anthem for the sixties generation: "Freedom's just another word for nothing left to lose."

Much of the success of the Brownsville-born Kristofferson must be attributed to his own personality, a charismatic aura that combines a rugged physical attractiveness with an astute intelligence. That personality took him to Hollywood in the seventies, but writing and performing still appear to be his first love, and he has revived his concert appearances on a regular basis. So the story of this itinerant Texan is far from over, and similarly, the story of a fellow Texan who possesses the same streak of individuality continues to unfold.

As Kristofferson gained entrance to the exclusive Nashville club of singer-songwriters, Willie Nelson was leaving it. Willie had achieved a degree of success as a songwriter since his arrival in 1959; his songs had been recorded by others and were consistently on the charts and occasionally at number one: *Crazy* (Patsy Cline), *Hello Walls* (Faron Young), *Hello Fool* (Ralph Emery), *Night Life* (Ray Price), *Family Bible* (Claude Gray), *I Never Cared for You* (Fred Foster). By the mid-sixties Nelson had scored several hits of his own, *Touch Me, Funny How Time Slips Away,* and *The Party's Over.* But by 1971, his career was at a standstill; Willie was pulling in one direction and the Nashville executives in another. He felt that he had lost control over his own music, so he left Nashville — it was the beginning of a new era for country music.

Willie Hugh Nelson was born on 30 April 1933 in Abbott, Texas. His musical education began early; his grandfather taught him guitar chords at the age of six. Before his eleventh birthday, Willie had landed a job playing rhythm guitar for a German polka band, and in high school he had his own group, featuring sister Bobbie Nelson on piano. Willie paid his dues working as a disc jockey for several years

Guy Clark was an integral part of the country-rock movement in Austin as well as being one of Nashville's finest songwriters. *(Brian N. Kanof.)*

Willie and Charlie Pride at Soap Creek Saloon in Austin, 1976. *(Scott Newton.)*

Waylon Jennings—from West Texas rockabilly to one of today's major country stars. *(Rick Henson.)*

in San Antonio, Fort Worth, and Pasadena, but he also found plenty of work playing gigs on weekends and writing songs. For a while he played bass in Ray Price's Cherokee Cowboys band, and that proved to be the connection that would give exposure to his songwriting talent.

Nelson's songs were universally admired—recorded by such diverse artists as Lawrence Welk, Stevie Wonder, Frank Sinatra, and B. B. King. He came from the second generation of Texas honky-tonkers, but the Nelson style had a unique melodic quality and phrasing that was lacking in the traditional honky-tonk sound. The lyrics were not complex or surreal, but like the Kristofferson songs, they possessed a depth of human emotion and compassion. Their beauty lies in their ability to come alive and take the listener along for a three-minute journey through Willie's mind and soul.

> **It's been rough and rocky traveling**
> **But I'm finally standing on the**
> **ground**
> **After taking several readings**
> **I'm surprised to find my mind's still**
> **fairly sound**
> **I guess Nashville was the roughest**
> **But I know I've said the same about**
> **them all**
> **We received our education**
> **In the cities of the nation**
> **Me and Paul.**

Willie and Paul (his long-time friend and drummer Paul English) had moved back to Texas in 1971, changed record labels, and by 1973 recorded the *Shotgun Willie* album in New York. Willie and his band (Paul on drums, Bobbie Nelson on piano, Bee Spears on bass, Jimmy Day on steel guitar, and later Jody Payne on guitar and Mickey Raphael on harmonica) took Austin by surprise—electrifying young rock-oriented crowds at the Armadillo World Headquarters. And then on 4 July 1973 the first Willie Nelson festival was held at Dripping Springs, twenty miles down the road from Austin; it was billed as the largest country music festival ever held. On succeeding fourth of July weekends for the rest of the decade, the size of the crowds at Willie's picnics paralleled his success and fame—they got larger and larger.

As the albums continued to dominate the country charts (*Phases and Stages, Shotgun Willie, Red Headed Stranger, Stardust,* and *The Outlaws*) Willie solidified his hold over the music-crazed audiences in Austin and Texas, but he also infiltrated the traditional country market. His versions of *Blue Eyes Crying in the Rain* (1976), *Always on My Mind* (1982), and *Poncho and Lefty* (1983 duet with Merle Haggard), rival the all-time sales records of any performances in the country music industry. Nashville had succumbed to the Nelson magic by the late seventies. The rhinestone and sequined Tennessee stars now let their hair grow a little longer, embraced rock with a sincere passion, and looked to Texas for the spirit of the new music, not to mention the dollar signs.

The press and the image makers tried to categorize Willie and those who joined him in the new alliance between rock and country, redneck and hippie. They were labeled "outlaws," and the music was called "progressive country." But in reality, the music defied categorization—it was simply Texas music. The basic Willie Nelson formula was traditional country steeped in the rock that had grown out of Texas' diverse ethnic heritage. Riding the success of that heritage alongside Willie was country music's most visible link to the early Texas rockabilly style, Buddy Holly's last bass player, Waylon Jennings.

W aylon Jennings was born in 1937 in Littlefield, a small town in the middle of the cotton country of the South Texas plains. His exposure to borderline Texas poverty and the music of Bob Wills and Ernest Tubb was reminiscent of Willie Nelson's upbringing. After

Billy Joe Shaver, one of the "Nashville rebels." *(Scott Newton.)*

Mac Davis—one of America's favorite entertainment personalities during the 1970s. *(Courtesy of Polygram Records.)*

John Denver's lyrics emphasized the relationship between traditional rural values and a respect for the environment. He was the most successful performer in American pop and country music during the mid-seventies. *(Courtesy of RCA Records.)*

Kenny Rogers in concert. Since 1977 Rogers has dominated the country-pop field. *(Rick Henson.)*

Barbara Mandrell — the queen of country-pop. *(Courtesy of MCA Records.)*

his years in Lubbock as a disc jockey and a rock 'n' roller with Buddy Holly, Waylon moved to Phoenix and began a career as a country-folk performer. In 1965 he made the move to Nashville, and as a successful studio musician and solo performer he recorded over twenty-five albums. Jennings even tried his hand with the movies, both acting and doing soundtracks. He won a Grammy in 1969 with a country version of *MacArthur Park*. Even though he continued to live in Nashville, Waylon bolted to the New York record companies following Willie's lead; the same independence surfaced, and the same desire to determine the direction of his own music rocked the old Nashville establishment.

The Willie-Waylon connection reached cult status within the Austin scene. The highlight of Willie's picnics arrived when Waylon joined Willie for a duet; they had become the heroes described so eloquently in their music. After the success of *The Outlaws*, their partnership on a record was a guarantee for a million-seller. The hit single, *Luckenbach, Texas*, came from Waylon's album *Ol' Waylon*, just one of his many giant album hits of the seventies (*The Ramblin' Man*, *This Time*, *Honky-Tonk Heroes*, *Lonesome, On'ry and Mean*, and *Dreaming My Dreams*). The Waylon Jennings' musical style and personality fit comfortably into the changing music scene in Austin; it was as if he had been waiting for years and now everyone else had arrived. Waylon's presence exuded a hard-living independence, a mystical attitude that he had done and seen it all. His music was straightforward country, yet always tinged with rock 'n' roll. And most importantly, there was a warmth, a shared experience of highs and lows that flowed between Waylon and his audience, other musicians, and of course, Willie.

Tanya Tucker has been a major country star since she was thirteen years old. Many of her hit songs reflect her Texas roots. *(Courtesy of MCA Records.)*

Sam Neely had several hits during the seventies. Today he is the dominant country-rock artist in the Corpus Christi area. Pictured with Neely is Rose Lantz. *(Author photo, Texas Music Collection.)*

Although threatening the old Nashville guard, the three towering figures in modern country music—Nelson, Jennings, and Kristofferson—revived country and brought it a new audience. A great many young Texans continued the trends set by the three leaders. Although most of that group remained in Austin, some tried Nashville, where they made it as singers or writers. Included in that array of "Nashville rebels" was Lee Clayton, Guy Clark, Mickey Newberry, Tony Joe White, and Billy Joe Shaver. The cowboy revival and the Texas chic of the mid-seventies fit perfectly with the public's image of the outlaw movement, and the songwriters did not miss the opportunity to make their lyrical comment. Waylon had a huge hit with Lee Clayton's *Ladies Love Outlaws*. And Billy Joe Shaver's *Willie the Wandering Gypsy and Me* also merged the spirit of the Old West with the nomadic life of a musician "on the road." Shaver had other hits with *Ride Me Down Easy*, *Old Five and Dimers Like Me*, and *I'm Just an Ole Lump of Coal*, but his finest lyrical effort was *Good Christian Soldier*. It was released by Kris Kristofferson and was the most moving, as well as most powerful antiwar song of the 1970s. The old Nashville elite would never have touched lyrics like Shaver's coupled with the raw, gut-level delivery of Kristofferson:

> **It's hard to be a Christian soldier**
> **When you tote a gun.**
> **And it hurts to have to watch a**
>   **grown man cry**
> **But we're playing cards, writing**
>   **home, having lots of fun**
> **Telling jokes and learning how**
>   **to die.**

The message conveyed to Nashville by the overwhelming commercial and artistic success of the Texans was that there is room for everyone in country music. Other Texans were making the same point from the pop-oriented side of the country music industry. Mac Davis of Lubbock had several crossover hits in the 1970s, such as *I Believe in Music*, *Baby Don't Get Hooked on Me*, and *Stop and Smell the Roses*. Davis' ventures into television and the movies often overshadowed his music, but he was a major influence in bringing pop styles to country audiences.

The most successful crossover performer of the seventies was country-folk artist John Denver. His career began during the folk era of the early sixties with various folk acts in Fort Worth and Lubbock. After a four-year stint with the Chad Mitchell Trio, Denver's first hit, *Take Me Home, Country Roads*, climbed to the top of both the pop and country charts. This breakthrough came on the heels of a gold record that he had written for Peter, Paul, and Mary, *Leaving on a Jet Plane*. Several Grammy Awards and gold records later (*Rocky Mountain High*, *Thank God I'm a Country Boy*, *Annie's Song*, and *Back Home Again*), Denver was the superstar of country-pop. Although his designation as "country" was resented by many Nashville types, his inclusion in that genre is just as valid as anyone who sings of the virtues of rural and mountain living. The mountains of Colorado are just as country as the hills of Tennessee. Perhaps Denver's message of environmental concern implied an activist commitment that conservative Nashville was unwilling to embrace.

John Denver opened the door for country-pop in the same

Mickey Gilley and Johnny Lee. *(Rick Henson.)*

Moe Bandy (left) and Joe Stampley. *(Rick Henson.)*

George Strait began his career with the country band Ace in the Hole in Central Texas. *(Courtesy of MCA Records.)*

manner that Willie and Waylon had opened it for country-rock. For the last several years the leader in the country-pop field has been another Texan, Kenny Rogers. Rogers started as a rock 'n' roller in the late fifties with a Houston band, the Scholars. They had a moderate hit (*That Crazy Feeling*), but Rogers moved on to play bass for the pop-jazz group, the Bobby Doyle Three. Then he joined the New Christy Minstrels just as the folk movement was reaching its commercial peak. Next, he led the First Edition, a rock group that did very well in the late sixties and had a major crossover hit with *Ruby, Don't Take Your Love to Town.* In a little over a decade, Rogers had tasted success in three different segments of the music industry, but the superstar status that he enjoys today did not come until the success of *Lucille* in 1977. The commercial achievements of Kenny Rogers, as well as his nearly endless number of Grammy Awards and Country Music Association Awards, have forever ended the old Nashville debates on the desirability of fusing country and pop. The sales figures of Kenny Rogers, John Denver, and their female counterpart, Barbara Mandrell, settled the argument faster than any discussions of musical purity or "country" integrity. Houston-born Barbara Mandrell has long been a part of mainstream Nashville, but it was not until she moved to more pop-oriented material

that her career took off. She followed the Mac Davis formula with her own television variety program and is the leading female performer in Nashville today. Barbara's sister Louise Mandrell has a thriving recording career as well.

The paucity of women in the music industry is a reflection of the repressive sexism that exists in all segments of American society. The training ground for most musicians has always been the clubs and taverns that until recent years were off limits for "decent" women. But the restrictions and the old prejudices are dying, and Texas women are playing a predominant role in the world of country music. Tanya Tucker, born in Seminole and raised in West Texas and California, has been one of the more visible Texas women in Nashville. She has been a star since the age of thirteen, and after a decade of hits (*Delta Dawn, What's Your Mama's Name, Would You Lay with Me, Texas When I Die,* and *San Antonio Stroll*), the little-girl image is gone. Her songs today are pure country-rock, a sure sign of success in the eighties. Tanya's sister LaCosta, Billie Jo Spears, Jeannie C. Riley, and Dottsy Brodt have also scored national hits. Riley, from Anson, had the biggest country hit of 1968, *Harper Valley P.T.A.* A large contingent of Texas women performers have roots in Austin; those with country orientations include Marcia Ball, Chris O'Connell, Dee Moeller, Katy Moffett, Lisa Gilkyson, Nanci Griffith, Kimmie Rhodes, Traci Lamar, and Karen Brooks. These Austin women are equally at ease performing rock, folk, or R and B, and each has played an integral role in the development of the Austin legacy to country music.

The list of Texans in country music is an exhaustive one. They come from every spot on the map; Johnny Bush from Houston, Sam Neely from Corpus Christi,

The Gatlin Brothers Band—(left to right: Rudy, Larry, and Steve). *(Courtesy of CBS Records.)*

Terry Stafford from Amarillo, Red Steagall from Gainesville, Buck White (and daughters Sharon and Cheryl) from Wichita Falls, Billy Walker from Ralls, Bob Luman from Nacogdoches, Charlie Walker and Boxcar Willie from East Texas, Johnny Duncan from Dublin, Johnny High from Grapevine, Johnnie Lee from Houston, Gene Watson from Palestine, Kenny Dale from Houston, Michael Ballew from Austin, Gary Morris from Fort Worth, George Strait from San Marcos, and Tommy Hancock (with his Supernatural Family Band) from Austin.

Down in Pasadena, Mickey Gilley rides herd over the urban cowboys in his showcase Texas honky-tonk. Long before *Urban Cowboy* brought his unique piano stylings to the movies, Gilley had a consistent string of honky-tonk hits. But he is at his best when he sings soft country ballads, such as *True Love Ways, You Don't Know Me,* and *That's All That Matters to Me.* Two other honky-tonkers join Gilley in the East Texas tradition of beer-drinking, working-class songs, Moe Bandy and Joe Stampley. From the other side of the state come the masters of today's country-pop sound, Larry Gatlin and the Gatlin Brothers Band. Larry, Rudy,

Two generations of the *conjunto* sound—Santiago Jiménez (left) on the accordion, and his son Flaco Jiménez (right) on the *bajo sexto.* Also pictured, on bass, Juan Viesca. *(Chris Strachwitz, Arhoolie Records.)*

and Steve Gatlin grew up in Odessa, and after Larry's success as a single, they united and became one of Nashville's dominant groups with hits like *Broken Lady, Take Me to Your Lovin' Place,* and *All the Gold in California.* Another West Texan who has been a steady hit maker for the last decade is Don Williams. His pure country ballads are vintage Texas—emotion-filled country poetry delivered with a smooth Texas drawl (*Amanda, I'm Just a Country Boy, Lay Down beside Me, Good Ol' Boys Like Me*). One of Williams' most notable performances and one of country music's classic recordings of the eighties was his duet with Emmylou Harris, *If I Needed You* (written by Austin writer Townes Van Zandt).

The ethnic exclusion in mainstream country music is an issue that has rarely concerned industry executives, but in Texas the ethnic diversity has created another reality. They are often labeled "folk" or "ethnic," but the tremendous number of performers that play in an isolated geographic or cultural region are "country" within their own realm. In Texas, the most graphic example, *conjunto* music, comes from the Mexican-American community. *Conjunto* (a Tejano band with fewer than six pieces, usually including an accordion and a twelve-string guitar called a *bajo sexto*) combines the *boleros, rancheros,* and waltzes from northern Mexico with the German and Czech polkas of Central and South Texas to form a dance music unique to the American Southwest. The old masters of *conjunto* (often called "Tex-Mex") include Narciso Martínez, Lydia Mendoza, Valerio

Don Williams has had a continual string of hits from his folk career in the sixties to his eighties role as country music's finest balladeer. *(Rick Henson.)*

Longoria, Mongo Saldívar, and the one-time king of them all, Santiago Jiménez. During the 1950s Tex-Mex groups like Beto Villa, Isidro López, and Los Alegres de Terán continued the tradition.

Today the "Rey de Acordeón" ("King of the Squeezebox") is Flaco Jiménez of San Antonio. Flaco has done more to export the Tejano style to worldwide audiences than any of his predecessors, having appeared on national television and toured and recorded with Ry Cooder and Doug Sahm. Other Tejano groups on the Texas circuit are Los Polkeros (Ben Tavera King and Frank Corrales), René Ornelas, Sunny Ozuna, Reuben Ramos, Río Jordan (Steve Jordan), and the favorites of the younger crowd of record buyers, Little Joe y la Familia, Mazz, La Mafia, Jimmy Edwards, Ramón Ayala, Lisa López, and Laura Canales. Little Joe Hernández has a strong following in Austin and has made an impact there the last few years with other Austin musicians who look to the *conjunto* style for much of their material and inspiration (Tomás Ramírez, Beto y los Fairlanes, Joe "King" Carrasco).

Cousins of the *conjunto* sound are the German and Czech polka bands that dot the small towns of Southeast and Central Texas. The oldest and most famous of the Czech bands is the Baca Band, led by Gil Baca. His grandfather formed the group in 1892, and the family has continued the tradition in Fayetteville without missing a Saturday night. Other polka bands include the Fritz Hodde Band, the Red Ravens, and a group led by Lee Roy Matocha, the leading radio broadcaster specializing in polka music. And, playing out of New Braunfels since 1949, the Hi-Toppers Orchestra remains one of the favorite German dance bands in the state.

Laura Canales is one of the major Tejano recording stars. *(Courtesy of Freddie Records.)*

A growing part of the local country music scene in Texas is the revival of bluegrass and old-time mountain fiddling. A renewal of interest in the Anglo-American origins of today's commercial music spurred the growth of numerous bluegrass and fiddlers' associations around the state. There are also a great many contests and special performances that celebrate the skills of the southeastern mountain folk heritage. A selection of those include the Texas State Fiddlers' Championships at Hallettsville, the World's Fiddlers' Contest at Crockett, the Harry Smith Old Time Fiddlers' Contest in Paris, bluegrass performances at Kerrville and the Bastrop Opera House, and the Texas Folklife Festival in San Antonio. Texas also boasts four of the finest bluegrass ensembles in the South: Grassfire, the Shady Grove Ramblers, the Leon Valley Boys, and Tennessee Valley Authority.

The major ethnic style in far Southeast Texas is "zydeco," the music of the Cajuns. It developed in the 1930s when French-speaking black and white musicians from Louisiana combined the hillbilly and honky-tonk country sounds with those of blues and jazz. Today zydeco is more rhythm and blues than country, but the emphasis on dance music has remained the same since its inception. The leading figure among the zydeco artists is Clifton Chenier, still playing out of Cajun country with his Red Hot Louisiana Band. Other prominent Cajun performers include groups like Buckwheat (Stanley Duval), Dopsie and the Twisters, and singer Link Davis, Jr.

Of all the performers who have come from the Texas reservoir of ethnic musical backgrounds, only two have crossed over into the mainstream country industry. They are Freddy Fender and Johnny Rodríquez. Fender (Baldemar Huerta) is from San Benito but now lives in Corpus Christi. He burst onto the country charts in 1975 with a Huey Meaux-produced record, *Before the Next Teardrop Falls.* Fender followed that up with *Wasted Days and Wasted Nights* and *Since I Met You Baby.* After enjoying tremendous crossover popularity in the mid-seventies, Freddy Fender is making a recording and touring comeback under the guidance of Huey Meaux.

Johnny (left) and Little Joe Hernández. *(Courtesy of Freddie Records.)*

Tara Turner and Dayton Roberts at the Texas Old Time Fiddlers' Contest—the tradition continues. *(Robyn Turner.)*

Johnny Rodríguez, Tex-Mex and country superstar. *(Rick Henson.)*

Freddy Fender was one of country and pop's major crossover artists of the 1970s. *(Rick Henson.)*

While Freddy Fender paid his dues for years in country, rock, and Tex-Mex, Johnny Rodríquez became a star in his early twenties. Rodríquez, from Sabinal, was discovered by Tom T. Hall while performing at Happy Shahan's Alamo Village near Brackettville. He has had songs on the country charts consistently for nearly ten years—hits like *Pass Me By*, *Love Put a Song in My Heart*, *North of the Border*, and *Ridin' My Thumb to Mexico*. Rodríquez brought a much needed youthful image to Nashville, and the fact that he was attractive and Chicano produced a lot of copy for the industry publicists. The talent of Rodríquez did not need the hype, however, and he continues to enjoy widespread popularity.

The publicity people also hit a bonanza when the daughter of one of Nashville's own (Johnny's daughter Rosanne Cash) married a young Texas singer-songwriter from Houston, Rodney Crowell. As it turned out, the publicity was justified; Crowell is the finest songwriter working in Nashville today. His own albums have done well, with songs like *Stars on*

Rodney Crowell and Rosanne Cash on "Austin City Limits," 1983. *(Photo by Scott Newton, courtesy of "Austin City Limits".)*

The Geezinslaw Brothers, Sammy Allred (left) and Dwayne Smith. *(Rick Henson.)*

Waylon and Willie.*(Rick Henson.)*

Leon Russell—one of the towering figures in American music. From his association with Willie Nelson to his innovations in country-rock, Leon has exerted a tremendous influence on the Texas sounds. *(Scott Newton.)*

Ray Wiley Hubbard—"Up against the wall redneck mother." *(Scott Newton.)*

the Water. But no one today is combining melody and lyrics with such mastery as Rodney Crowell. His songs are fast becoming Texas classics: *'Till I Gain Control Again* (recorded by Crystal Gale and Jerry Jeff Walker), *On the Banks of the Old Bandera* (by Jerry Jeff Walker), and *Shame on the Moon* (by Bob Seeger).

Country music in the 1980s bears little resemblance to that first country recording by Eck Robertson in 1922. Today there are lush sound studios, million-dollar contracts, electronic instruments, and the prevailing influences of rock and pop—but the people remain the same. And the hopes and frustrations that fill their songs are the same human emotions that carried Americans across the Texas frontier.

However, country music is no longer the sole province of the rural society with its tenacious adherance to older, conservative traditions. The Texans changed that and helped bring the country message to a younger, urban audience. The new Texas frontier lies in its cities.

The rapid changes in country music have generated fear and criticism among many who value the older country imagery. But what is country music and what is not country music is a concern that exists in the corporate boardrooms of Nashville—not with the Texas musicians. As Kris Kristofferson observed, "If it sounds country, then it is." The real danger of country music disappearing or blending into a homogenized version of pop occurs when the labels, the promotion, and the money take precedence over the art. In Texas, the music comes first.

♫

Jerry Jeff and Jesse Walker. *(Courtesy of MCA Records.)*

10
The Austin Legacy

I want to go home with the Armadillo

I want to go home with the Armadillo
Good country music from Amarillo
and Abilene
The friendliest people and the prettiest
women
You've ever seen.

London Homesick Blues
Gary P. Nunn

The musical diversity that has flowered in Texas for a century and a half found a home in the 1970s—Texas rhythm and Texas rhyme came full circle in Austin. As a social phenomenon, the music of that period not only brought together divergent lifestyles and philosophies, but it also left a thriving legacy of musical freedom and experimentation. The musicians and their audience reached back into a rich Texas past and removed the boundaries and restrictions that plague much of American popular music. As a result, Austin became and remains the most dynamic musical city in the United States—a creative oasis where rock, rhythm and blues, folk, country, and jazz all share power in a musical democracy.

Most attempts to define the Austin musical renaissance of the seventies usually violate the spirit of that era with generalizations and simplistic categorizations. When the public and the press became aware that a "movement" was in progress, the labels surfaced. Some called it "progressive country," others proclaimed it "redneck rock," many decried it as "outlaw" music. Perhaps at first, it was simply the merging of two apparently incongruous sounds and lifestyles— country and rock.

Country-rock fusion began in California in the late six-

ties, with Bob Dylan, Gram Parsons, and the Byrds originating the process. But the movement did not gather momentum until Nashville began to feel the effects after the Austin musical community demonstrated that basic rock roots were the wave of country music's future. If Austin music began as a "new" or "progressive" appendage of country, it soon evolved to represent much more than a record company press agent could capsulize in a catchy phrase. The state capital evolved into a musical showcase exhibiting 150 years of Texas social history.

Even though Austin has always been a pocket of creativity amidst the political conservatism and social conformity that rule Texas, music never rivaled education or politics as the lifeblood of the city. That slowly began to change during the 1960s—the decade when America's commitment to social justice and equality came of age. Much of the idealism of that period sprang from the college campuses, and after the idealism faded to reality in the early seventies, Austin and the University of Texas remained one of the few places where the dream continued. There was a certain naïveté in that dream, but the musicians who migrated to Austin and displayed a passion for social and musical change possessed the perfect blend of innocence, talent, and determination.

The first Willie Nelson picnic at Dripping Spring, Texas, 4 July 1973. *(Burton Wilson.)*

Gary P. Nunn in performance on "Austin City Limits," 1982. *(Photo by Scott Newton, courtesy of "Austin City Limits.")*

T here was a vibrant club scene in Austin as early as the mid-sixties when the folk craze was king of the campus at America's large universities. Kenneth Threadgill's service station-bar-honky-tonk served as headquarters for any aspiring folk or blues singer, the most notable graduate of that crew being Janis Joplin. Small clubs and coffeehouses intermittently rivaled the UT Student

Union as an alternative for both music and lifestyle. The environment surrounding the Austin live music clubs changed rapidly from 1965 until 1970—fraternity hang-outs became hippie dens overnight. There was the Jade Room, the New Orleans Club, the Eleventh Door, the One Knite, and music entrepreneur Rod Kennedy's Chequered Flag. The club most symbolic of the late-sixties acid rock era was the Vulcan Gas Company. The Vulcan gave credence to Austin's reputation as a wide open, experimental community where young minds would face establishment-threatening values. But there was little philosophy or political rhetoric to be found at the Vulcan Gas Company; it mainly served up heavy doses of Texas rock 'n' roll. Its headliners were usually local bands like Roky and the Thirteenth Floor Elevators, Shiva's Headband, and Conqueroo, but occasionally blues greats such as Mance Lipscomb or Lightnin' Hopkins would be on the bill.

After the Vulcan closed its doors in 1970, an Austin trio (Eddie Wilson, Jim Franklin, and Mike Tolleson) became the guiding forces behind the single most important music hall in Austin's, if not the entire state's, history. The Armadillo World Headquarters opened for business in the summer of 1970. For the next ten years the Armadillo delivered Texas music with a personality true to its namesake—fiercely independent, oblivious to the abuse coming its way, and always moving with deliberate speed in no particular direction. The Armadillo was soon christened the creative home of Austin music, and indeed, its role was more than symbolic. It was the location where Willie Nelson first revealed his country magic to a predominantly young, rock-oriented audience. It did focus national attention on Austin after live recordings there by Freddie King, Waylon Jennings, and Commander Cody hit the top of the charts. And it was the most visible spot in Austin where country, rock, jazz, R and B, and even an occasional ballet, coexisted in a nebulous mixture of sounds called "Austin music."

Willie Nelson's endorsement by the Armadillo crowd was coupled with another event that helped build Austin's growing reputation as a national music center, the Willie Nelson Fourth of July picnics. The picnic at Dripping Springs in 1973 began the annual musical and social celebration that dur-

Michael Murphey, 1982. *(Photo by Scott Newton, courtesy of "Austin City Limits.")*

114

ing the next decade scattered Austin music and controversy all over the Central Texas map, from Gonzales to Liberty Hill to College Station. Willie's picnics were a strange combination of exhilaration and frustration. The array of talent and the energetic crowds produced a rush of excitement that the alcohol and marijuana could never rival. Willie's old Nashville friends joined the new contingent from Austin and charmed as many as 100,000 Texans during the three-day happenings beneath the broiling sun. But by the late seventies the problems of production, security, and financing

Doug Sahm at the Continental Club in Austin. To Sahm's left is his long-time friend and keyboard wizard, Augie Meyers. (*Author photo, Texas Music Collection.*)

Frummox (Steven Fromholz and Dan McCrimmon). This was the publicity photo for their 1969 album, *Here to There* — a collector's item today. (*ABC Records, courtesy of Steven Fromholz.*)

Kinky Friedman — "He's proud to be an American." (*Scott Newton.*)

115

Bobby Bridger performing his narrative epic, *Ballad of the West.* (*Robyn Turner.*)

Steven Fromholz—an Austin singer and songwriter who has few equals charming and entertaining an audience. (*Brian N. Kanof.*)

Three of Texas' finest songwriters (left to right: Kinky Friedman, Townes Van Zandt, and Billy Joe Shaver). (*Author photo, Texas Music Collection.*)

became unmanageable, and the concert series became another legend in Austin's rapidly evolving music scene.

The other major festival born in the early seventies, Rod Kennedy's Kerrville Folk Festival, is still alive and ranks among the finest in the country. The Kerrville Festival has grown to be a two-week affair every spring, featuring folk, country, bluegrass, and country-rock music. The secret to the success of Kerrville lies in Rod Kennedy's skilled promotion, the dedication of a group of inspirational musician-directors (Bobby Bridger, Steven Fromholz, Gary P. Nunn, Carolyn Hester, Allen Damron, Don Sanders, David Amram, and Peter Yarrow), and the spirit of Texas music exemplified by thousands of "Kerrverts." Kennedy continues to expand the events at his Quiet Valley Ranch near Kerrville throughout the summer with classical, jazz, and bluegrass festivals. There is an emotional aura that surrounds the Kerrville experience—a lump-in-the-throat and tear-in-the-eye warmth that never fails to peak when the audience sings the Kerrville theme song, Bobby Bridger's *Heal in the Wisdom:*

> ***There is a reason, there is a rhyme***
> ***There is a season and there is a time***
> ***There is a purpose and there is a***
>   ***plan***

And one day together we'll heal in the wisdom and we'll understand.

Other factors contributed to the sense of "musical community" growing in 1970s Austin. New radio formats, particularly KRMH and KOKE, expanded playlists to include a blend of country and rock. Under the leadership of DJs Rusty Bell and Joe Gracey, KOKE-FM led the rise of experimental radio in Austin. The KOKE format initiated the label "progressive country," and well over half of the music played came from Austin, or at least Texas, musicians. Joining the outdoor festivals and the new radio was a live music scene seething with excitement and creativity. The Armadillo may have been the pacesetter, but other clubs on the Austin circuit had a cult of devoted followers and each developed its own unique personality. There were Castle Creek, Soap Creek Saloon, the Saxon Pub, the Texas Opry House, and the old country reliables, the Broken Spoke and Split Rail. But it was the people who made the music—music laced with a down-home idealism devoted not only to the revived Texas spirit of individualism, but also to a 1960s' vision of communal integrity.

If Willie Nelson was the elder statesman of the Austin contingent, then Jerry Jeff Walker was surely next in command. Jerry Jeff was originally from upstate New York, but by the time he settled in Austin in 1971 he was more Texan in appearance, speech, and spirit than many lifelong residents. Known primarily as a folk singer in the sixties, Jerry Jeff came to epitomize the country-rock merger that was incubating in Austin bars in 1971 and 1972. Up to that time, Jerry Jeff was best known as the composer of *Mr. Bojangles*, a giant pop crossover hit recorded by everyone from Bob Dylan to Sammy Davis, Jr. Its message was as simple as its melody was beautiful; there is dignity in every human being. The first Austin albums by Jerry Jeff produced a number of songs that have been identified as symbolic of the "Austin sound." Among them were *Gettin' By*, *Sangria Wine*, *Charlie Dunn*, *Up against the Wall Redneck Mother* (written by Ray Wiley Hubbard), *L.A. Freeway* (by Guy Clark), *Desperados* (by Guy Clark), and *London Homesick Blues* (written and sung by Gary P. Nunn). They leaned toward country on record, but in live performance they came out rock 'n' roll.

Over the next decade Jerry Jeff Walker achieved the largest national following of that first wave of Austin musicians (excepting Willie Nelson). He was the hard-drinking, hard-living character about whom he often

Townes Van Zandt at a 1983 taping of Austin City Limits. *(Photo by Scott Newton, courtesy of "Austin City Limits."*

sang. Today there is still nothing quite like the emotion and music of a Jerry Jeff concert. Even though he devotes his energy in the eighties to his good health instead of to his self-destruction, Jerry Jeff Walker creates the finest example of country-rock to be found anywhere. The imitators in Nashville have yet to capture his flair and magic.

Part of the Jerry Jeff magic came from his backup group in the mid-seventies, the Lost Gonzo Band. There was no more talented aggregation of Austin sidemen, and they eventually became one of Austin's favorite bands after leaving Jerry Jeff to strike out on their own. Their ranks consisted of Gary P. Nunn, Bob Livingston, John Inmon, Kelly Dunn, and Donny Dolan. Some of Austin's finest entertainers played behind Jerry Jeff and were members of the Lost Gonzo at various times, musicians such as Craig Hillis, Michael

Willis Alan Ramsey in performance at the Kerrville Folk Festival. *(Brian N. Kanof.)*

Country music columnist for the *Austin American-Statesman*, Townsend Miller (left) and Kerrville music promoter, Rod Kennedy. *(Brian N. Kanof.)*

Bill and Bonnie Hearne at the Kerrville Folk Festival, 1983. *(Brian N. Kanof.)*

McGeary, Herb Steiner, Mickey Raphael, and Tomás Ramírez. All of the former Gonzo members are still active musically in the 1980s.

Of all that talented pool, Gary Nunn has proved to be one of Austin's most prolific and most successful songwriters. His *London Homesick Blues* was the official anthem for Texas music of the seventies—the plea of a wayward poet who finally realizes that his roots and future lay in his native Texas. Other Nunn songs have made it to the national charts—*Couldn't Do Nothin' Right* (by Rosanne Cash) and *The Last Thing I Needed* (by Willie Nelson). Gary Nunn is the consummate Austin musician—superb songwriter, sincere singer, and an infectiously good-time entertainer.

Most of the Lost Gonzo Band began their Austin careers

Allen Damron, one of the guiding forces behind the Kerrville Folk Festival and one of its featured entertainers. *(Brian N. Kanof.)*

Carolyn Hester, Texas' premier folk singer, 1982. *(Brian N. Kanof.)*

backing another dominant contributor to Texas music in the 1970s, Michael Murphey. Murphey grew up in Dallas, attended North Texas State University, and spent the late 1960s working as a songwriter for Screen Gems in Los Angeles. It was a rejection of all those experiences that drew him to Austin; a quick listen to a few of his introspective song lyrics reveals the reasons for his move. From his first album, *Geronimo's Cadillac,* Murphey's nonthreatening intellect and piercing social conscience were evident in his work. He delivered the perfect blend of poetic imagery and activist philosophy to a generation that desperately wanted to believe that the sixties mattered. There was the ultimate environmental statement in *Boy from the Country;* America's moral bankruptcy was exposed in his collaborative work with Charles John Quarto, *Geronimo's Cadillac; Calico Silver, Cherokee Fiddle,* and *Good-bye Old Desert Rat* explored the dignity of the nineteenth-century hero; the simple beauty of nature was eloquently described in *Wildfire* and *Swans Against the Sky;* and the frustrating search for identity was illuminated in *Blessing in Disguise* and *Michael Angelo's Blues.* Michael Murphey expressed in one line the postsixties syndrome that was felt by thousands of young Texans, "I'm on a southwestern pilgrimage where

Nanci Griffith writes and sings some of today's most moving and beautiful music. *(Brian N. Kanof.)*

Perhaps more than any one factor, it was song lyrics that distinguished the Austin sound. No matter if the music had a country twang or rock 'n' roll pulse, the lyrics embodied an intellect absent in the Nashville formula and an emotion that could compete with any hard-metal rock rhythm. No one in town translated the Texas folk-rock-country tradition into words better than Steven Fromholz. Fromholz, like Michael Murphey, a recruit from the folk-rock scene at North Texas State, is a master entertainer — weaving wit and insight into a mini-monologue that separates the songs that make you laugh from the songs that make you cry. Among his many quality songs (*I'd Have to Be Crazy, Dear Darcie, Isla Mujeres*), his *Texas Trilogy* stands as the classic Texas folk song of this century. *Texas Trilogy* is a narrative ballad that brings to life the suppressed conflicts faced by Texans as they moved from a rural to an urban society. It relates with vivid reality the twentieth-century Texas frontier of small towns tied together by a disappearing railroad. The song displays a special feeling and respect for the women who built this state with their strength and patience. The combination of personality and lyrical skill as evidenced in *Texas Trilogy* make Steven Fromholz one of America's most expert verbal craftsmen.

Another Austin musician combines the beauty of a poet with the insight of a historian. Bobby Bridger is usually described as a folk singer, but that label neglects the urgency

the middle class can't run me down no more."

Most of Michael Murphey's success in the seventies and eighties has come on the country charts, but he has had several crossover hits into pop and rock. His versatility makes it difficult to pin on a commercial label. The same irony applies to the Texas artist with the most diverse collection of musical talents, Doug Sahm. The reason Sahm has escaped national acclaim and media attention is his refusal to turn his career over to a record company publicist. Sahm has been one of Texas' most accomplished performers since his Sir Douglas Quintet rock 'n' roll days of the mid-sixties. Often joined by his San Antonio sidekick, Augie Meyers, Doug Sahm still plays the most entertaining mix of rock, R and B, country, and Tex-Mex from Austin to San Francisco to Amsterdam.

The most colorful, if not controversial, of the Austin musicians is Texas' own "singing Jewboy," Kinky Friedman. Kinky (or Richard, as he is known by long-time Austin residents) has also had problems with identification — his lyrics turn off traditional country fans and his style and instrumentation seldom approximate rock. But for those who love his message — the hypocritical and pretentious people and institutions in our society should be exposed — Kinky is a rare talent and a genius at social commentary. With songs like *Sold American, They Ain't Making Jews Like Jesus Anymore, Ride 'Em Jewboy,* and *People Who Read People Magazine,* nothing and no one is immune from the Friedman satire. Along with his musical skills, Kinky Friedman possesses another commodity that is unusual in the world of American popular music — a heavy dose of honesty.

B. W. Stevenson — "Buckwheat" in performance, 1982. *(Brian N. Kanof.")*

as well as the timeless quality of his music. His ballads do speak of the past—mountain men, Indians, explorers of another age—but Bridger's musical message looks forward; he sings of those, past or present, who seek harmony with nature. Bridger has faced the dilemma of trying to sell music with noncommercial themes to a public that often views serious reading as a quick glance through the TV log. But Bobby Bridger has and will endure with entertaining and inspiring songs like *The Call, Seekers of the Fleece,* and *Heal in the Wisdom.*

Other descendants of the early sixties folk revival and the subsequent folk-rock era joined the Austin musical community. Rusty Wier, one of the few native Austinites in that group, had previously been in bands like Lavendar Hill Express and Rusty, Layton, and John, before going solo. Wier's act was pure country-rock, but his Texas style and imagery cast him in the country mold more than many of his contemporaries. He had a hit with *Don't It Make You Wanna Dance* and had several good album sales, particularly *Stoned, Slow, and Rugged.* But Wier's real talent—charming a Texas crowd—was best witnessed in a rowdy Austin bar whenever Wier broke into his infamous *I Heard You Been Layin' My Old Lady.*

Other important members of the Austin crowd were Townes Van Zandt, a country-folk performer whose writing skill is today bringing him national recognition with hits for Emmylou Harris, Don Williams, and Willie Nelson; Willis Alan Ramsey, the composer of a brilliant album containing memorable songs like *Northeast Texas Women, Boy from Oklahoma, Painted Lady,* and *Goodbye Old Missoula;* and B. W. Stevenson, one of the younger Austin singers whose crystal-clear vocals brought him action on the national charts with *My Maria* and *Shambala.* B. W. was another one of the arrivals who came to Austin by way of Dallas and North Texas State. Other members of the Austin family included Milton Carroll, Doak Snead, guitar aficionado Kurt Van Sickle, the country-folk duo Bill and Bonnie Hearne, Tim Henderson, Allen Damron, and Ray Wiley Hubbard.

As the reputation of Austin spread nationwide, hundreds of musicians poured into the city looking for a one-night

A long-time member of the Austin music scene, folk-rock-country performer Rusty Wier. *(Brian N. Kanof.)*

stand or the chance to latch on to an established band. And what an assortment of bands there were: country-rockers like Greezy Wheels, Plum Nelly, Three Faces West, Whistler, Ewing Street Times, Mother of Pearl, and Balcones Fault; and western-swing bands led by Alvin Crow and the Pleasant Valley Boys, Asleep at the Wheel, Buckdancer's Choice, and Ace in the Hole (with George Strait). And there was Freda and the Firedogs—playing an occasional rock or blues number between their traditional country standards. Freda was Marcia Ball, the premier woman performer in the

The Uranium Savages. *(Courtesy of George and Carlyne Majewski.)*

Stevie Ray Vaughan (left) and Paul Ray performing at Soap Creek Saloon, Austin. *(Photo by Ken Hoge, courtesy of Diana and Paul Ray.)*

Freda and the Firedogs (left to right: David Cook, Steve McDaniels, Marcia Ball, Bobby Earl Smith, and John Reed). *(Burton Wilson.)*

The Fabulous Thunderbirds (left to right: Jimmie Vaughan, Kim Wilson, Keith Ferguson, and Fran Christina). *(Dennie Tarner.)*

Angela Strehli (left) and Marcia Ball—two of the major performers who led the evolution of Texas music in the seventies and eighties. *(Dennie Tarner.)*

Austin crowd. From her very first show at the Tiger Lounge in Baton Rouge, Marcia embodied all the skills and styles prevalent in the Texas music heritage. She can rock 'n' roll, wail a country ballad, or sing the blues with southern emotion. There were other women breaking into the male-oriented club of Texas music (Dee Moeller, Chris O'Connell, Lisa Hattersley, Mary Egan, Karen Brooks, Lucinda Williams, and Nanci Griffith), but none commanded the stage presence and the unpredictable versatility of Marcia Ball. She is more blues-oriented today, but Marcia is still Austin's favorite.

Throughout the seventies more quality bands appeared—bands that more often than not defied description because of their diverse material and the freedom allowed them by the Austin audience. There were the Cooder Browne Band (with Larry Franklin), Too Smooth, Austin All-Stars, Balcones Fault, St. Elmo's Fire, Ain't Misbehavin', Eaglebone Whistle, Grimalkin, Uncle Walt's Band, and the Uranium Savages.

The continual migration of musicians led to a second wave of talent in the late seventies, a wave that blew in off the South Texas plains. The Lubbock connection to Texas music has always been something of a mystery, or at least a consistent topic of discussion over a beer when the band takes a break. But the reality of Lubbock's contribution was never more apparent than when Austin became the home of Joe

Backstage at Antone's—(left to right: Kim Wilson, Fran Christina, Sarah Brown, and Albert Collins). *(Susan Antone)*

122

Stevie Ray Vaughan, America's most exciting guitarist. *(Scott Newton.)*

Butch Hancock, the West Texas poet whose lyrics celebrate Texas culture. *(Brian N. Kanof.)*

The Jazzmanian Devil, Tomás Ramírez. *(Photo by Jim McGuire, courtesty of BBA Management.)*

Joe Ely, performing his unique brand of West Texas rock, 1983. *(Scott Newton.)*

The Next at the New Wave Fest, 1979 (left to right: Arthur Hayes, Ty Gavin, Lee Shup). *(David Fox.)*

Ely, Butch Hancock, and Jimmie Gilmore. Their story begins in Lubbock during the mid-sixties with a group called the T. Nickel House Band (with members Jimmie Gilmore, Joe Ely, John Reed, Jesse Taylor, and Tiny McFarland). After a reshuffling of members, they showed up in Austin as a rock group called the Hub City Movers. A final reincarnation became the Flatlanders (Ely, Gilmore, and Hancock). By the mid-seventies, their solo careers began to take off—

careers that still provide Texas' most eloquent songwriting and dynamic singing.

The songwriting is vintage Texas, or at least, vintage West Texas—songs like Gilmore's *Dallas from a DC-9* and *Treat Me Like a Saturday Night*, and Ely's *I Had My Hopes Up High*, *Honky Tonk Masquerade*, and *All My Love*. But it is Butch Hancock who is the master poet. His songs are textbook versions of symbolism and word play, always incisive and reflective of his West Texas experience. Some of Hancock's best include *If You Were a Bluebird*, *Two Roads*, *Tennessee's Not the State I'm In*, *One Road More*, *West Texas Waltz*, *You've Never Seen Me Cry*, and the song that conveys a special message to any male Texan who came of age in the sixties, *She Never Spoke Spanish to Me*:

**She said, ''If you're from Texas,
   son,
Then where's your boots
And where's your gun?''
I smiled and said, ''I got guns
No one can see.''**

Butch Hancock will someday break through his regional success to nationwide recognition with his lyrical skills. Joe Ely has already achieved that recognition with his charismatic style and his ability to tap the deep roots of rock 'n'

Beto y los Fairlanes (Robert Skiles at the piano). *(Photo by Scott Newton, courtesy of BBA Management.)*

roll. For a brief period Ely was only considered a country-rock or West Texas rockabilly performer. But after his last albums (*Musta Notta Gotta Lotta* and *Live Shots*), and after witnessing one of his exhausting performances, there is little doubt that Joe Ely is genuine Texas rock 'n' roll—and the best proponent of that evolving legacy begun by Buddy Holly. The Holly ghost apparently motivated a whole generation of Lubbock youth. Other contemporaries of Ely and Hancock who have contributed to the Lubbock mystique include Terry Allen, David Halley, and one of the fastest-rising groups in the state, the Maines Brothers.

Joe Ely is representative of many Texas artists in the mid-seventies who traveled full circle in their musical repertoire. They grew up on rock, moved into folk and folk-rock, discovered country, and dabbled in country-rock before returning to a broader definition of rock 'n' roll. Similarly, there was a growing trend in Austin during the seventies that reached back even farther—all the way back to rock's foundation, rhythm and blues. The nucleus of Austin R and B consisted of artists like Paul Ray, W. C. Clark, Angela Strehli, and the Vaughan brothers (Jimmie and Stevie Ray). Paul Ray had experimented with R and B back in the late sixties with a Dallas-based blues band, 1948, and later his group, the Cobras, became Austin's hot rhythm and blues act for several years. In the mid-seventies, when country-rock was dominant, clubs like Antone's and the Rome Inn were about the only blues outlets in Austin, but several bands and individuals made it through that rough era.

One of those groups was Hard Times, later known as Southern Feeling. Angela Strehli, W. C. Clark, and Denny Freeman—all prominent Austin blues artists—came from that association. Two other important bands were Steam Heat and Storm, which, along with Paul Ray, was composed of other important members of the Austin blues community, Jimmie Vaughan, Ed Vizard, and Lewis Cowdrey. And

The LeRoi Brothers at Hut's, Austin. *(Chuck Gist.)*

there was also the Triple Threat Revue (Stevie Ray Vaughan, W. C. Clark, Lou Ann Barton, with Mike Kindred). By the early eighties, two bands dominated the Austin, and Texas, blues scene, Stevie Ray Vaughan and Double Trouble and the Fabulous Thunderbirds. Double Trouble had originally consisted of Stevie Ray and Lou Ann Barton, who along with Angela Strehli and Marcia Ball are today the headline blues singers in town. Before his tragic death in 1990 Stevie Ray Vaughan was regarded as one of America's preeminent guitarists. His brother Jimmie Vaughan joins Kim Wilson and their fellow Thunderbirds as one of America's best rhythm and blues bands, credentials that come from no less than the Rolling Stones, with whom they have toured.

Today the R and B community in Austin has spread its talent and its impact statewide. Traditional bluesmen like Johnny Copeland, Johnny "Guitar" Watson, Robert Ealey, Blues Boy Hubbard, and Albert Collins have a wider range of club opportunities than ever before.

Joe King Carrasco on "Austin City Limits," 1981. *(Photo by Scott Newton, courtesy of "Austin City Limits.")*

Joe King Carrasco and El Molino at Raul's in Austin, 1979. (left to right: Speedy Sparks, Richard Elizondo, Joe King). *(David Fox.)*

Rank and File (left to right: Alejandro Escovedo, Chip Kinman, Tony Kinman, Slim Evans). *(Photo by Bill Daniel, courtesy of Carlyne Majewski and Slash Records.)*

D-Day (left to right: Glover Gill, Will Fiveash, John Keller, De Lewellen, and David Fore). *(Courtesy of Moment Productions.")*

The great diversity of blues-oriented performers has never been more apparent, from the country-blues sound of Lucinda Williams to the blues-funk of Extreme Heat. There are also the reggae and Third World artists such as the Lotions, Pressure, Beto y los Fairlanes, and the unique St. Croix Philharmonic.

Another important musical and social development surfaced in the late 1970s, the new wave movement. Having grown out of a rejection of disco and the fact that mainstream rock was now very establishment, new wave sought change in both musical style and personal imagery. The change in music was basically a return to earlier rock rhythms—in many ways some sort of strange hybrid between rockabilly and psychedelia. The personal trappings in appearance and attitude were a bit more complex and varied from individual to individual as to their statement. New wave touched only a few places in Texas, and surely Austin was the center with clubs like Raul's, Duke's, and Club Foot. There were some notable groundbreaking groups appearing in those spots in the late seventies—the Violators (with Jesse Sublett and Kathy Valentine of the Go-Go's), the Next (with Ty Gavin), the Huns, and Terminal Mind.

As any social or musical movement evolves, new terminology and imagery develop to meet the requirements of growing or dying. Such is the case with new wave. It had its punk subculture, and today new descriptive labels have arrived, terms such as "hardcore" and "new music." The reality of the music is a simple one—it's still rock 'n' roll. Among the hundreds of new wave groups on the Texas scene, some of the more prominent are Standing Waves, the Big Boys, D-Day, Jitters, Private Lives, X-Spand-X, and the Lift.

On the fringe of the new wave designation are many of the eighties' various adherents to Texas rock 'n' roll—bands like the Explosives, the Skunks, neofunk groups like Random Culture, experimental bands such as the Pool (Patrick Keel), country-rockers like Rank and File, and the most nationally renowned of the Texas contingent, Joe King Carrasco. Joe King grew up in Dumas on the northern edge of the Texas Panhandle, worlds away from his memorable performances at Austin's Club Foot or his sold out successes all across South America. His first Austin band, El Molino, eventually gave way to today's internationally known Joe King Carrasco and the Crowns. The Carrasco sound is somewhere between Tex-Mex rock and new wave fun, with a little African and Texas funk thrown in. Perhaps the best

Charlie Sexton, a leader of the new generation of Texas rock 'n' roll. *(Rick Henson.)*

Eric Johnson—the guitar talents of Johnson were first observed in the mid-seventies jazz-rock group the Electromagnets. *(Photo by Mary Beth Greenwood, courtesy of Rock Arts.)*

description is Austin music, 1980s' version.

A resurgence of good-time rock 'n' roll seems to be the agenda for the 1980s. The rockabilly revival that began in 1980 shows no sign of disintegrating. Actually, it grows steadily stronger with bands like the LeRoi Brothers, Charlie Sexton and the Eager Beaver Boys, the Rock-a-Dials, the Trouble Boys, Johnnie Dee and the Rocket 88s, and Whoa! Trigger. Other varieties of rockers can be found statewide— the Van Wilks Band, Vince Vance and the Valients, Johnny Reno and the Sax Maniacs, Jesse Sublett's Secret Six, Stephen Doster, Bugs Henderson, Roky Erickson, and Texas' most accomplished rock guitarist, Eric Johnson. And the national rock stars (ZZ Top, Steve Miller, Johnny and Edgar Winter) are still contributing to the innovations and versatility that characterize Texas rock in the eighties. Two performers who have captured that rock versatility and are on the verge of a national breakthrough are Houston's Shake Russell and Austin's Eliza Gilkyson.

Whether it be rock 'n' roll, country, jazz, or rhythm and blues, there is no longer much distinction between Austin music and Texas music in the 1980s. The state has followed the lead of the Austin musical community by expanding its concept of what is musically and artistically acceptable. The music could be at Poor David's Pub or the Deep Ellum section of Dallas, Rockefellers in Houston, the St. Mary's district in San Antonio, on Sixth Street or at Antone's in Austin—the labels matter little to the audiences; they only demand quality

Extreme Heat (left to right: Phill Ritcherson, Eddie Cantú, Mike Barnes, Vince Bryant, Neil Pederson, and Bruce Spelman). *(Photo by Jan Butchofsky, courtesy of Mike Barnes.)*

The Armadillo World Headquarters was demolished in 1981 to make way for a high-rise office building and hotel complex; however, you cannot tear down an idea or kill a spirit. The Armadillo lives. *(Art work on the Armadillo mural by Henry Gonzales, author photo, Texas Music Collection.)*

Shake Russell (left) and John Vandiver at the Kerrville Folk Festival, 1982. Russell also teamed with another Texas performer for several years, Dana Cooper. Known in Texas for his quality vocals, Russell is rapidly gaining a national reputation as composer of a number of beautifully crafted songs like *You've Got a Lover* and *Deep in the West*. *(Brian N. Kanof.)*

music. For nearly twenty years the Austin emphasis on experimentation and innovation has reinforced the old cliche that there are only two kinds of music, good and bad. The Austin legacy symbolizes this tradition of quality and diversity that has characterized a century and a half of Texas music.

Eliza Gilkyson's southwestern roots are reflected in the wide range of her musical talents. Gilkyson is pictured here in performance at emma-joes in Austin, 1983. *(Carrie Robertson.)*

ZZ Top—entering their third decade as the leaders of Texas rock 'n' roll (left to right: Billy Gibbons, Dusty Hill, and Frank Beard). *(Photo by George Craig, courtesy of Bill Narum)*

Epilogue

I will be waiting for my brave companion of the road

*When the lights go down
and the dance floor is empty
and the crowd is going home
. . . I will be waiting
for my brave companion of the road.*
Brave Companion of the Road
Nanci Griffith

As the cultural phenomenon known as "Texas music" enters the new decade of the 1990s, it remains an elusive and nebulous concept. Everyone has a definition that vaguely fits his or her own image of what it means to be "Texan." This is perhaps a frustration for those who desire simple categorizations and dependable stereotypes, but it is the ambiguity of "Texas music" that provides its beauty and power. That theme runs throughout the first ten chapters of this book as diversity and change dominate the historical overview. This Epilogue serves a similar purpose—to pictorially update the vast array of Texas musical talent.

Some of the performers in this Epilogue are survivors, those whose careers have endured and led them to national recognition. Others are relatively new musicians whose national exposure is just beginning. Like those talented people who fill the pages of this book, these Texas artists and their music have taken Americans in two divergent,

yet very compatible musical directions. They have taken us backward and revived a historical awareness of that mother lode of the Texas heritage, our ethnic diversity. But they have also taken us forward to an awareness that music can serve as a progressive movement where no barriers of class or race or sex restrict the creative spirit.

From that idealistic perspective, "Texas music" exists as a social phenomenon capable of defining a future vision of what Texas might possibly be—an egalitarian Texas stripped of chauvinistic myth and false pride. As music has paralleled our political and social maturity as a people, it has proved to be a powerful democratic weapon, possessing the strength to inspire the intellect and sensitize the heart. But even if that visionary potential falls short, the music will survive. And we will all be better for it, "for the good times."

Lefty Wilbury, alias Roy Orbison, in concert at Austin City Limits. *(Scott Newton)*

The solo career of Don Henley skyrocketed in the late 1980s. In addition to the commercial success of his concerts and music videos, Henley finally achieved the critical acclaim that was often missing during his glory days with the Eagles. *(Photo by Mathew Rolston, courtesy of Geffen Records)*

Edie Brickell and the New Bohemians (far right to left: Brad Houser, John Bush, Matt Chamberlain, Wes Burt-Martin, Edie Brickell, and Kenny Withrow). *(Photo by Paul Natkin, courtesy of Geffen Records)*

Timbuk 3—Barbara and Pat MacDonald. *(John Carrico)*

Michelle Shocked at the Ballad Tree, Kerrville Folk Festival. *(John Carrico)*

Steve Earle continues to defy the media image makers as he challenges the definitions of country and rock. *(Photo by Scott Newton, courtesy Austin City Limits)*

Sara Hickman in performance in 1990 on Austin City Limits. *(Photo by Scott Newton, courtesy Austin City Limits)*

San Antonio's pop-rock sensation, Michael Morales. *(Photo by Andrew W. Long, courtesy Benson-Vale Management)*

Will and the Kill (left to right: Jeff Boaz, Will Sexton, Alex Napier, and Thierry LeCoz). *(Scott Van Osdol, courtesy of Lone Star Silver)*

Award winning songwriter and singer, Tommy Pierce. *(Courtesy of Tommy Pierce)*

Michael E. Johnson and the Killer Bees (left to right: Lonnie Hutchinson, Michael E. Johnson, Ishmael Sealy, Wallace Hammond, Jerry Stevens, and Brian Weinstein). *(Jeff Rowe, courtesy of Lone Star Silver)*

Michael Slattery and Todd Kassens (of Shoulders), Kris McKay, and Susan Voelz—in performance at the South by Southwest musical showcase in Austin, 1990. *(John Carrico)*

Poi Dog Pondering *(Jeff Rowe, courtesy of Lone Star Silver)*

Versatile rock 'n' roller, Alejandro Escovedo *(Photo by Shannon McIntyre, courtesy of DiMenno Productions)*

Blues-rock artist, Chris Thomas *(Photo by John DeLeon, courtesy of the Dianne Scott Agency)*

Music journalist John T. Davis (far right) observes Lubbock's famed country rockers, the Maines Brothers. *(John Carrico)*

A major "country" star by the late 1980s, Lyle Lovett in performance at Gruene Hall. *(John Carrico)*

Kelly Willis and Radio Ranch had their career launched by a performance at the South by Southwest music festival in Austin (left to right: David Murray, Michael Hardwick, Kelly Willis, Mas Palermo, and Brad Fordham). *(Photo by Mark Guera, courtesy of Carlyne Majer, ATS Management)*

Houston's Clint Black emerged in 1990 as the brightest new star on the country scene. *(Courtesy of Lone Wolf Management)*

Originally from San Antonio, Holly Dunn had great success in the late 1980s from her Nashville base. *(Photo by Randall Wallace, courtesy of Warner Brothers Records)*

Little Joe Hernandez has had a thirty year career that has ranged from traditional Tejano music to rhythm and blues, from country to rock and roll. *(Clay Shorkey)*

George Strait—country superstar of the 80s and 90s. *(Photo by Mike Rutherford, courtesy of MCA Records)*

The South Texas supergroup—the Texas Tornados (left to right: Flaco Jimenez, Augie Meyers, Doug Sahm, and Freddy Fender). *(Photo by Mark Guerra, courtesy Warner Brothers Records)*

The Highwaymen—Willie Nelson, Waylon Jennings, Johnny Cash, and Kris Kristofferson. *(Rick Henson)*

Winner of three Grammy Awards, nationally acclaimed Asleep at the Wheel (left to right: Ray Benson, John Ely, Tim Alexander, Michael Francis, Jon Mitchell, David Sanger, and Larry Franklin). *(Photo by Mark Seliger, courtesy Benson-Vale Management)*

The two Texas stars who have expanded the boundaries of country music, Lyle Lovett and Ray Benson. *(Rick Henson)*

The Wagoneers (left to right: Monte Warden, Tom Lewis, Craig Pettigrew, and Brent Wilson). *(ATS Management)*

Ray Benson "boogies back to Texas." *(John Carrico)*

George Strait and Johnny Gimble in performance on Austin City Limits (left to right: Richard Casanova, Benny McArthur, Johnny, George, Rick McRae, and Roger Montgomery). *(Rick Henson)*

George Strait joins Leon McAuliffe at an Austin City Limits salute to Bob Wills and the Texas Playboys. *(Rick Henson)*

Alvin Crow and fiddle, 1990. *(Jane Stader)*

Rosie Flores at Kerrville. *(Photo by Bob Talbot)*

Al Dressen introduces Cliff Bruner at the 1989 ceremony inducting Bruner into the Western Swing Hall of Fame (left to right: Chris O'Connell, Cliff Bruner, Al Dressen, and Paul Glasse). *(Photo by Hans Otto, courtesy of Al Dressen)*

Jerry Jeff Walker at Gruene Hall, 1990. *(Photo by Jim McGuire, courtesy of Tried and True Music)*

Still "going home with the armadillo," Gary P. Nunn entertains audiences from Europe to Texas and all across America. *(Jane Stader)*

Michael Martin Murphy, based in northern New Mexico, has had great success with the Nashville country audiences singing his songs of love and his ballads of the Southwest. *(Merri Lu Park)*

Despite expanding his career with writing and acting projects, Bobby Bridger is at his best singing tales of the American West. Here he leads a Kerrville Folk Festival audience in the singing of his inspiring anthem, *Heal in the Wisdom. (Jane Stader)*

Now known to the public as a famous mystery novelist, Kinky Friedman remains a "faded, jaded, fallen cowboy star" to his devoted fans. *(Brian Kanof)*

Willis Alan Ramsey and Alison Rogers, backstage at Kerrville, 1990. *(John Carrico)*

Eliza Gilkyson's songwriting and singing abilities take her from folk to country to rock 'n' roll. *(Brian Kanoff)*

Butch Hancock and Jimmie Dale Gilmore *(Brian Kanof)*

Bill Oliver spreads a message of environmental consciousness with his music. *(Photo by Scott VanOsdol, courtesy of Lone Star Silver)*

Singer and songwriter, Christine Albert *(Jeff Rowe, courtesy of Lone Star Silver)*

Tish Hinojosa has taken her folk ballads of West San Antonio to a nation-wide audience. *(Photo by Scott Newton, courtesy Austin City Limits)*

Darden Smith. *(Photo by Melodie Gimple, courtesy of Benson-Vale Management)*

David Halley *(John Carrico)*

Nanci Griffith emerged as a national star in the late 1980s. Here she is performing at the Kerrville Folk Festival. *(Jane Stader)*

Joe Ely *(Jim Schwenke)*

Jesse Taylor and Butch Hancock. *(John Carrico)*

Omar and the Howlers (left to right: Bruce Jones, Omar Dykes, John Inmon, and Gene Brandon). *(Jeff Rowe, courtesy of Lone Star Silver)*

Mel Brown (left), Hubert Sumlin, and Barbara Lynn playin' the Texas blues. *(Susan Antone)*

Lavada Durst (Dr. Hepcat), Roosevelt T. Williams (the Grey Ghost), and Erbie Bowser—the Texas piano professors, proponents of the Texas "barrelhouse blues." *(Clay Shorkey)*

Delbert McClinton, the master of Texas honky-tonk rhythm and blues. *(Scott Newton)*

Angela Strehli (left) and Lou Ann Barton. *(Susan Antone)*

W. C. Clark and his Blues Revue. *(Chuck Gist)*

Carmen Bradford—jazz vocalist with the Count Basie Orchestra. *(Photo by Jeff Rowe, courtesy of Lone Star Silver)*

Dancing at Hut's in Austin during the mid-1980s—Charlie Sexton and Lou Ann Barton. *(Chuck Gist)*

Albert Collins (left) and Kim Wilson in performance at Antone's in Austin. *(Susan Antone)*

Houston bluesman, Johnny Copeland. *(Photo by Robert Turner, courtesy of Texas Music Collection)*

Jimmie Vaughan-Clifford Antone-Stevie Ray Vaughan *(Susan Antone)*

Jimmie Vaughan (right) and his replacement with The Fabulous Thunderbirds, Duke Robillard. *(Susan Antone)*

Stevie Ray Vaughan—a Texas legend, never to be forgotten. *(Dennie Tarner)*

Bibliographic Essay

The historical community has never treated music as a topic worthy of serious scholarship and research. Usually viewed as merely an appendage of cultural history, music in Texas has especially fallen victim to a brand of academic elitism. The traditional volumes and textbooks on Texas history rarely give music more than a one-page treatment, and often that brief account only mentions a few prominent musicians in the classical field or on the Broadway stage. And even the trade publications that focus on the commerical aspect of American popular music have failed to produce one book totally dedicated to Texans and their musical heritage. Perhaps this general survey of Texas music will help reverse that trend and accelerate interest in this integral facet of Texas social history. The following bibliographic notes detail the sources for this book as well as highlight the available material necessary to begin any analysis of American popular music.

The Nineteenth-Century Tradition

The nineteenth-century folk music tradition in Texas has been included in numerous studies of American, southern, and southwestern folklore. A starting point in discovering the regional folk heritage of the American people is the Alan Lomax anthology, *Folk Songs of North America* (New York: Doubleday and Company, 1960). Lomax combines his collection of major folk songs with an analysis of their origins and their relationship to social and cultural factors. For the location of specific topics and studies, the best source is the bibliographic work by D. K. Wilgus, *Anglo-American Folksong Scholarship since 1898* (New Brunswick, N.J.: Rutgers University Press, 1959). The most insightful and complete study of the southern folk tradition is *Southern Music, American Music* (Lexington: University Press of Kentucky, 1979), by Bill Malone. Malone not only traces the evolution of southern folk music into the various twentieth-century pop styles, he explores the commercialization of southern music and the resulting effects. Other general volumes that include Texas and southern folk music are *A History of Popular Music in America* (New York: Random House, 1948), by Sigmund Spaeth; *An Introduction to Folk Music in the United States* (Detroit, Mich.: Wayne State University Press, 1960), by Bruno Nettl; and *Folk Song: U.S.A.* (New York: Duell, Sloan, and Pierce, 1947), by John A. Lomax and Alan Lomax.

As for specified studies on Texas folk songs, two books by William Owens are the most informative, accurate, and entertaining. Owens has spent a lifetime collecting and analyzing the varied ethnic folk experiences unique to Texas in *Texas Folk Songs* (Dallas: Texas Folklore Society, 1950), and his recently published *Tell Me a Story, Sing Me a Song* (Austin: University of Texas Press, 1983). Other complementary works on Texas folk music include Lota Spell's *Music in Texas* (Austin: privately printed, 1936), Martha Anne Turner's *The Yellow Rose of Texas* (Austin: Shoal Creek Publishers, 1976), and the songbook of Texas-Mexican folk songs along the lower border region, *A Texas-Mexican Cancionero* (Urbana: University of Illinois Press, 1976), by Américo Paredes.

The most respected books on black folk music are *The Music of Black Americans: A History* (New York: W. W. Norton, 1971), by Eileen Southern; *The Negro and His Folklore in Nineteenth Century Periodicals* (Austin: University of Texas Press, 1967), edited by Bruce Jackson; *Black Culture and Black Consciousness* (New York: Oxford University Press, 1977), by Lawrence Levine; and *Sinful Tunes and Spirituals: Black Folk Music to the Civil War* (Urbana: University of Illinois Press, 1977), by Dena Epstein. All of these sources emphasize African and slave-society origins of black folk music, but they also relate the effects of that music to the political and social perceptions embraced by the modern black community. The major bibliographic collection on black folk music and its commercial offspring is *Afro-American Folk Culture: An Annotated Bibliography of Materials from North, Central, and South America and the West Indies* (Philadelphia: Institute for the Study of Human Issues, 1977), edited by Roger Abrahams and John Szwed.

There are a number of studies on ragtime music and the ragtime era which bridged the gap between the music of the slave culture and modern popular music. Those works include *They All Played Ragtime* (New York: Oak Publications, 1971), by Rudi Blesh and Harriet Janis; Edward Berlin's *Ragtime: A Musical and Cultural History* (Berkeley and Los Angeles: University of California Press, 1980); and *Rags and Ragtime* (New York: Seabury Press, 1978); by David Jasen and Trebor Jay Tichenor.

The major figure of the ragtime era, Scott Joplin, has recently begun to be studied in great detail. Two important books on Joplin and his role in the flowering of American popular music are Peter Gammond's *Scott Joplin and the Ragtime Era* (New York: St. Martin's Press, 1975), and *Scott Joplin* (Garden City, N.Y.: Doubleday and Company, 1978), by James Haskins and Kathleen Benson.

Early Country

The most complete and scholarly study of country music is the highly respected *Country Music, USA* (Austin: University of Texas Press, 1968), by Bill Malone. Originally his doctoral dissertation at the University of Texas, Malone's book is now recognized as the standard reference for any analysis of country music. It traces the evolution of country traditions in the seventeenth and eighteenth centuries all the way through the latest stylistic changes that affected country music into the 1960s. A companion volume is *Stars of Country Music* (Urbana: University of Illinois Press, 1975), edited by Bill Malone and Judy McCulloh. The lives and careers of several Texans are highlighted in this look at the contributors to the modern country scene (Eck Robertson, Vernon Dalhart, Ernest Tubb, Tex Ritter, Johnny Rodríquez).

Two other important sources on country music follow an encyclopedia format, with personal sketches and short essays on particular topics. Those are *The Country Music Encyclopedia* (New York: Thomas Crowell Company, 1974), by Melvin Shestack, and *A History and Encyclopedia of Country, Western, and Gospel Music* (Nashville: McQuiddy Press, 1961), by Linnell Gentry.

The rise of country music as a commercial enterprise is best documented in *The Illustrated History of Country Music* (Garden City, N.Y.: Doubleday and Company, 1980), edited by Patrick Carr, and *Just Country* (New York: McGraw-Hill, 1976), by Robert Cornfield. There are other invaluable surveys of country that include excellent picture collections, such as Robert Shelton's *The Country Music Story* (New York: Bobbs-Merrill, 1966), and Douglas Green's *Country Roots: The Origins of Country Music* (New York: Hawthorn, 1976). Both are informal histories, but both contain provocative insight and interesting factual material. Another unique approach to understanding the origins of country inspiration can be found in *Sing Your Heart Out, Country Boy* (New York: E. P. Dutton Company, 1975), by Dorothy Horstman. It is filled with lyrics to many of the classic country songs and corresponding essays describing their origin and composer.

There are two major archives for country music in the United States at present, the Country Music Foundation and Museum in Nashville, and the John Edwards Foundation at UCLA in Los Angeles. However, smaller historical repositories are beginning to appear everywhere on a regional basis.

The Singing Cowboys

The first collection of native Texas cowboy songs was the John A. Lomax anthology, *Cowboy Songs and Other Frontier Ballads* (New York: Sturgis and Watson, 1910). Lomax later added another volume, which described his over-forty-year search for Texas frontier music, *Adventures of a Ballad Hunter* (New York: Macmillan Company, 1947). There are also a great number of the Texas cowboy ballads included in his son Alan's *Folk Songs of North America*.

Each of the following books on country music contains a separate chapter on the singing cowboy and his role in the development of the country music industry: Carr's *The Illustrated History of Country*, Shelton's *The Country Music Story*, and Cornfield's *Just Country*. Bill Malone also offers a fairly in-depth analysis of the cowboy image and the growth of "western" music in *Country Music, USA*.

The best full-length treatments of the singing cowboys and the related music of the American West are *Cowboys and the Songs They Sang* (New York: William Scott Company, 1967), by S. J. Sackett; *The Singing Cowboys* (San Diego: A. S. Barnes and Company, 1978), by David Rothel; and *Git Along, Little Dogies: Songs and Songmakers of the American West* (Urbana: University of Illinois Press, 1975), by John White.

The Country Blues

The most complete scholarship on the country blues and their origins has been done by Samuel Charters. His works contain a sociological perspective that other blues books lack. Charters' accounts of the Texas country blues experience are in *The Country Blues* (New York: Rinehart, 1959) and *The Bluesmen* (New York: Oak Publications, 1967.) A more detailed study of the African tradition and the evolution of the blues through the slave culture can be found in *The Story of the Blues* (New York: Barrie, 1969), by Paul Oliver.

The cultural borrowing between black and white musicians and its effect on American popular music is the topic of Ortiz Walton's *Music: Black, White and Blue* (New York: William Morrow, 1972). This cultural exchange and the resulting impact of black society on American music is more fully explored in *Blacks, Whites, and Blues* (New York: Stein and Day, 1970), by Tony Russell, and *Early Downhome Blues* (Urbana: University of Illinois Press, 1977), by Jeff Titon.

The finest example of a primary source on the country blues is a collaborative effort by A. Glenn Myers and Texas bluesman Mance Lipscomb. Myers has compiled an extensively detailed and excellently researched biography on the life of Lipscomb. Interviews and thoughtful insights compose the bulk of *I Say Me for a Parable: The Life and Music of Mance Lipscomb*, a masterpiece of oral history.

One of the major repositories of blues recordings and pictures is Arhoolie Productions in El Cerrito, California. The founder of Arhoolie, Chris Strachwitz, has spent over twenty years assembling his collection of ethnic music. In regard to Texas, that collection includes the major Texas country bluesmen and blueswomen as well as the *conjunto* music of the Texas-Mexican community.

Western-Swing

Western-Swing is usually viewed as an appendage of country music, and as such, it is usually addressed in one or more chapters by the surveys of country music. The best accounts of western-swing in Texas can be found in the previously discussed books by Patrick Carr *The Illustrated History of Country Music*), Robert Shelton (*The Country Music Story*), and Douglas Green (*Country Roots: The Origins of Country Music*).

Any serious study of western-swing must concentrate on its central character, Bob Wills. Several Wills biographies have appeared over the years, including Ruth Sheldon's *Hubbin' It: The Life of Bob Wills* (Tulsa: privately printed, 1938), and *My Years with Bob Wills* (San Antonio: Naylor

Company, 1976), by Al Strickland with Jon McConal. But the most thorough, as well as entertaining, biography of Bob Wills is the landmark work by Dr. Charles Townsend, *San Antonio Rose: The Life and Music of Bob Wills* (Urbana: University of Illinois Press, 1976). Townsend's book is one of the first serious scholarly treatments on a popular musician, and as such, it has opened the door for more extensive research on the effects that American popular music figures have had on social and cultural history.

Jazz and the Big Bands

Jazz has attracted more literary attention than any form of American music. Among the valuable surveys and general reviews on jazz are the *Who's Who of Jazz: Storyville to Swing Street* (New York: Chilton Book Company, 1972), by John Chilton; *The Encyclopedia of Jazz* (New York: Horizon Press, 1966), by Leonard Feather; and *A Pictorial History of Jazz* (New York: Crown Publishers, 1955), by Orrin Keepnews and Bill Grauer, Jr. A more in-depth study of the sociological implications of jazz and its origins can be found in *The Story of Jazz* (New York: Oxford University Press, 1970), by Marshall Starns, and *Jazz: A History* (New York: W. W. Norton, 1977), by Frank Tirro.

The best analysis of the Texas jazz scene and the territorial bands of the Southwest is Ross Russell's *Jazz Style in Kansas City and the Southwest* (Berkeley and Los Angeles: University of California Press, 1971). Biographies on Jack Teagarden also offer an excellent portrayal of the inherent difficulties that jazz musicians faced in Texas during the early years, works like *Jack Teagarden: The Story of a Jazz Maverick* (London: Cassell, 1960), by Jay Smith and Len Guttridge, and *Jack Teagarden's Music* (Stanhope, N.J.: W. C. Allen Company, 1960), by Howard Waters, Jr. Another important study on Teagarden and his contemporaries is Albert McCarthy's *Big Band Jazz* (London: Barrie and Jenkins, 1974).

Rhythm and Blues

There are two major historical documentations of the evolution of the country blues to the modern era of R and B, Charles Keil's *Urban Blues* (Chicago: University of Chicago Press, 1966), and Arnold Shaw's *Honkers and Shouters: The Golden Years of Rhythm and Blues* (New York: Macmillan Company, 1978). Analysis of rhythm and blues from the broader context of Afro-American tradition is found in *Black American Music* (Boston: Crescendo Publishing, 1973), by Hildred Roach. A more political perspective on the blues is addressed by LeRoi Jones in his *Blues People: Negro Music in White America* (New York: Morrow and Company, 1963). Perhaps the most insightful study of the blues and the psychological importance they play in the black community is Robert Palmer's book *Deep Blues* (New York: Viking Press, 1981).

A number of books that focus on blues origins (mentioned in the chapter on the country blues) also have specific sections on the modern era of electrified and urban blues. These include Tony Russell's *Blacks, Whites, and Blues*, Paul Oliver's *The Story of the Blues*, Ortiz Walton's *Music: Black,*

White and Blue, and Samuel Charters' *The Bluesmen*.

Rock 'n' Roll

Rock 'n' roll is beginning to rival jazz as a subject worthy of social and political analysis. There are three serious histories on rock that focus on these aspects in correlation with the music: *The Story of Rock* (New York: Oxford University Press, 1969), by Carl Belz; *Sound Effects: Youth, Leisure, and the Politics of Rock and Roll* (New York: Pantheon Books, 1981), by Simon Frith; and *The Sound of the City: The Rise of Rock 'n' Roll* (New York: Dell Publishing, 1972), by Charles Gillett. The most widely read and without question the best overall survey of rock is *The Rolling Stone Illustrated History of Rock and Roll* (New York: Random House, 1976), edited by Jim Miller. This pictorial history has chapters on the "Texas sound" in rock as well as separate chapters on Buddy Holly, Roy Orbison, and Janis Joplin.

The massive amount of material available on rock lends itself to an encyclopedic approach. Two of the best volumes of that nature, full of trivia and biographical sketches, are *Rock On: The Illustrated Encyclopedia of Rock 'n' Roll* (New York: Thomas Crowell Company, 1978), by Norm Nite with Ralph Newman, and the *Encyclopedia of Pop, Rock, and Soul* (New York: St. Martin's Press, 1974), by Irwin Stambler.

Some of the more unusual rock studies include Michael Bane's review of the black origins of rock, *White Boy Singin' the Blues* (New York: Penguin Books, 1982); a political perspective of the folk-rock movement by R. Serge Denisoff, *Great Day Coming: Folk Music and the American Left* (Urbana, University of Illinois Press, 1971); and a cultural view of the rock singer as American hero in *Minstrels of the Dawn* (Chicago: Nelson-Hall, 1976), by Jerome Rodnitzky.

The two major Texas figures in rock have been interpreted by John Goldrosen's *Buddy Holly, His Life and Music* (Bowling Green, Oh.: Popular Press, 1975), and *Buried Alive* (New York: W. Morrow, 1973), a biography of Janis Joplin by Myra Friedman.

Modern Country

The last twenty-five years of country music are documented in specific chapters by Robert Cornfield in *Just Country*, Patrick Carr in *The Illustrated History of Country Music*, and Douglas Green in *Country Roots: The Origins of Country Music*. Bill Malone's *Country Music, USA* only extends into the mid-sixties, but an updated version is expected soon.

Contemporary interpretations of the country scene can be found in Nick Tosche's *Country: The Biggest Music in America* (New York: Dell Publishing, 1977); John Grissim's *Country Music: White Man's Blues* (New York: Coronet Communications, 1970); and Michael Bane's *The Outlaws* (New York: Country Music Magazine Press, 1978). One of the more innovative of the current books on country music is *You're So Cold I'm Turnin' Blue* (New York: Viking Press, 1982), by Martha Hume. Hume combines her personal perspective and insight with a vast collection of trivia and factual material.

Two other studies on modern country emphasize the rise of Nashville as a music center, but individual Texans receive extensive recognition in that development: *The Nashville Sound: Bright Lights and Country Music* (New York: Simon and Schuster, 1970), by Paul Hemphill; and *Nashville's Grand Ole Opry* (New York: Abrams, 1975), by Jack Hurst.

The Austin Legacy

The only full-length book to date on Austin music is *The Improbable Rise of Redneck Rock* (Austin: Heidelberg Publishers, 1974), by Jan Reid. Each of the dominant figures in that musical movement of the early seventies is featured in biographical sketches. Reid also evaluated the possibility and desirability of the emergence of Austin as a future musical center rivaling Nashville and Los Angeles. Another view of the Austin scene as simply an offshoot of traditional country music is the pictorial essay by Michael Bane, *The Outlaws* (New York: Country Music Magazine Press, 1978). Almost every book on popular music published after 1975 discusses Austin music and its phenomenal evolution and growth, usually as part of a chapter on country-rock.

Since Austin music, and correspondingly, the music of the rest of Texas, is still in flux and seems as though it will continue the dynamic change of the last decade, the best accounts of the current music developments are found in journalism. The *Austin Chronicle* and the *Austin American-Statesman* are two excellent sources that follow the evolving music scene in Austin and statewide.

Index